I0616101

FELICIA CARTRIGHT

AND THE
STORM-SCARRED MOUNTAIN

FELICIA CARTRIGHT

AND THE
STORM-SCARRED MOUNTAIN

BERNARD PALMER

ANEKO
PRESS

Felicia Cartright and the Storm-Scarred Mountain
© 2025 by Bernard Palmer
All rights reserved. First edition 1961.
Second edition 2025.

Please do not reproduce, store in a retrieval system, or transmit in
any form or by any means – electronic, mechanical, photocopying,
recording, or otherwise, without written permission from the
publisher.

Scripture quotations from The Authorized (King James)
Version. Rights in the Authorized Version in the United
Kingdom are vested in the Crown. Reproduced by permission
of the Crown's patentee, Cambridge University Press.

Cover Artwork: Adobe Firefly and Ideogram
Editor: Charlene Miskimen

Aneko Press *Youth*

www.anekopress.com

Aneko Press, Life Sentence Publishing, and our logos are trademarks of
Life Sentence Publishing, Inc.
203 E. Birch Street
P.O. Box 652
Abbotsford, WI 54405

JUVENILE FICTION / Religious / Christian / Action & Adventure

Paperback ISBN: 979-8-88936-298-2

eBook ISBN: 979-8-88936-299-9

10   9   8   7   6   5   4   3   2   1

Available where books are sold

CONTENTS

Ch. 1: He Wasn't the One 1

Ch. 2: The Ride to Laupen 9

Ch. 3: Mystery in the Air 17

Ch. 4: A Visit to the Award Room 29

Ch. 5: The Promise of Mountain Climbing 39

Ch. 6: The Story is Told at Last 49

Ch. 7: Two Clues but No Help 63

Ch. 8: Forgetting One's Burden to Help Another 71

Ch. 9: Puzzling Initials 83

Ch. 10: The Search Begins 91

Ch. 11: A Near Tragedy – A Teaching Appointment 105

CHAPTER 1

HE WASN'T THE ONE

Felicia Cartright and Joan Bailey stepped off the elevator to the main floor lobby, their bags in their hands. A bellboy, thin faced and graying, hobbled over to them.

"Checking out, Mademoiselle?" he asked Felicia, taking the case she was carrying.

"*Oui,*" she answered, "as soon as our friend comes down."

He took Joan's suitcase as well, staggering a bit under the load. "Won't you sit down?"

"Thank you."

They went over to a sofa facing the big glass doors and sat down.

It was snowing outside, a fine, powdery snow that filled the air and swirled along the street with each caprice of the breeze that whisked in off ice-bound Lake Geneva.

"Reminds me of home," Joan said, "and of all the work we'll have to make up when we get there."

A smile lifted one corner of Felicia's delicately shaped mouth. "If you'd been studying like the rest of us, you wouldn't have to worry so much when we get back."

Joan's shoulders shrugged. "Oh well, it'll work out some way. It always does."

"Much to Miss Duncan's surprise," Felicia added.

Joan Bailey chuckled. "You know, I think she's slightly amazed whenever I get a passing grade."

Felicia looked at her watch once more. "Speaking of Miss Duncan," she said, "where do you suppose she is? She told us she wanted to meet us here in the lobby at 9:30 sharp."

"Don't worry, she'll be along," Joan said. "I've been trying to lose her at every stop, but no such luck."

"You shouldn't talk that way, Joan," Felicia countered. "Miss Duncan has been a real sport on this choir tour. And when she decided to take an extra week and come over here to visit Miss Coulter before going back to America, she asked you and me to come along. She wouldn't have had to do that. The others are back in school by this time."

The bantering smile left Joan Bailey's face. "I'm really joking," she said. "Miss Duncan is a good scout. I don't know what Wellington would do without her."

The girls leaned back and lapsed into silence. Felicia closed her eyes momentarily. She opened them in time to see a tall, dark-haired young woman, a little older than herself, pause at the hotel doorway and speak softly to the St. Bernard dog she had on a leash. The big animal dropped obediently to the sidewalk almost at the doorman's feet.

"Look at that beautiful dog, Joan," Felicia whispered.

But somehow her attention was drawn irresistibly from the St. Bernard to his mistress who had entered the lobby. She was tall and slightly built, a willowy, sweet-featured young woman, tastefully but inexpensively dressed. Her face seemed made for laughter, but her eyes were as soft, luminous, and sad as those of her pet.

For an instant or two, she stood just inside the door, surveying the lobby. Then she started forward. A squat, poorly dressed woman about Miss Duncan's age, who obviously did not have a room at the hotel, got up and came to meet her. "Yvette! I'm so glad you came."

"Aunt Esther!" She kissed her affectionately on the cheek.

"I know you've only got a moment, but I had to talk to you," she said in French.

The girl called Yvette took the older woman by the arm tenderly and guided her to a sofa not far from where Felicia and Joan were sitting.

"I would like to stay a day or so with you, Auntie," Yvette replied, "but I have an appointment the first thing in the morning."

"I know, my dear. I know." The older woman took her young companion's soft fingers in her own work-roughened hand. "It was when you wrote that you were going up to Alpine Vista that I knew I had to talk with you first."

"Alpine Vista?" Joan whispered in Felicia's ear. "Isn't that where we're going?"

Felicia Cartright nodded and looked away. "I thought you used to boast that you had taken French two years and didn't understand a word," she said guardedly.

"That was back in Wellington," Joan retorted brightly. "Understanding this French is fun, especially when no one knows you understand it."

"Joan Bailey. You ought to be ashamed of yourself." She looked at Joan impishly. "Are you?"

Before Joan could reply, the girl spoke again.

"What is it, Aunt Esther?" she asked. The words seemed to come reluctantly and with some hesitation, as though she feared the answer but had to have it. "Why are you so anxious to see me before I go up to the school?"

"It is about your father."

"I suspected as much." Her gaze grew distant, and her hands worked nervously with her scarf.

Felicia saw the pain in her eyes, and her own heart ached for her.

"I was alone with him just before he died," the

older woman said. Her voice thinned and broke uncertainly.

The muscles in Yvette's throat tightened, and the lines around her eyes and the corners of her mouth deepened. She moved as though to speak, but her words were lost.

"He said he wasn't the one," Aunt Esther pronounced. "He said he didn't do it."

Yvette's arms straightened, and she dropped the scarf to the floor.

"He–he wasn't?" she echoed incredulously. It was as though the words had stolen her strength, leaving her weak and trembling.

"Those were his dying words."

The two women stared at one another. The silence around them was electric.

Felicia and Joan caught themselves leaning forward, listening intently.

"Aunt Esther," Yvette asked in syllables that were scarcely audible, "why didn't you tell me that b-b-before, instead of letting me think the worst all these years?" There was no anger in her voice, no accusation, only a question.

Suddenly Aunt Esther looked tired. Felicia and Joan saw strain in her pallid face. There was a weariness there that drove to the very marrow. "Perhaps I should have told you," she said, "but there was no proof." The lines in her face seemed to etch deeper. "And when I talked with the doctor, he said it could have been the delirium of a tortured conscience; your father's struggle within himself."

The words were a whiplash in Yvette's face. She winced. "Why do you tell me now?"

Aunt Esther clenched her fists until the cords on the backs of her hands showed white. "The answer is up there somewhere," she said. "Someone knows he isn't guilty. Don't you see? Someone up there knows the truth!"

That was the last either Joan or Felicia heard.

Miss Duncan got off the elevator, sweeping past the bellboy who reached for her bag, and came bustling over to where the girls were sitting.

Miss Duncan was flustered; there was no doubt of that. Her hair, still well-groomed for anyone except herself, was as close to being disheveled as the girls had ever seen it. Her jacket, usually meticulous in every detail, had the second button unfastened, and the collar was slightly wrinkled. It was only a crease to be sure, but a wrinkle, nevertheless.

Joan Bailey saw those things and smiled inwardly. "Never thought I'd see Miss Duncan breaking the cardinal rules of Wellington good grooming," she whispered to Felicia as the dean of women came pounding to a stop beside them.

"I'm dreadfully sorry," she exclaimed. "I had a phone call at the last moment, and I could not very tactfully end the conversation."

Felicia Cartright glanced beyond her at Yvette and

her aunt who were just going out the door. Yvette turned, took the older woman's hand briefly and patted it. Then she wiped at her eyes, spoke a word to the St. Bernard dog lying obediently near the door, and went up the street. The big dog was at her heels, his massive head at her fingertips.

"I am so sorry I'm late," Miss Duncan repeated.

"That's quite all right," Felicia answered. "We've enjoyed ourselves a great deal here."

Miss Duncan glanced at her watch, and the tension melted away. "There is plenty of time to catch our train."

Her gaze moved with studied calculation over the lobby and rested momentarily on a huge plate glass mirror on the opposite wall that reflected her person. Almost effortlessly, her hand came up to pat a single strand of hair into place and dropped to secure the offending button. The wrinkled collar yielded to the unobtrusive pressure of thumb and forefinger. Miss Duncan became herself again, prim, correctly groomed, and completely self-assured.

"If you girls will wait here," she said, "I shall go over and attend to the formalities of checking out."

"You know," Joan said to Felicia while Miss Duncan was at the desk, "I didn't think she'd ever get shaken up like that. I figured we'd see the Rock of Gibraltar flustered before we'd ever find Miss Duncan that way."

Felicia nodded disinterestedly. "What I'm concerned about right now is that girl who was here a few minutes ago," she said, keeping her voice low. "Did you see that look on her face?"

"What do you suppose is troubling her?" Joan Bailey asked.

"I wouldn't know," Felicia answered, "but it must be something terrible. I don't know that I've ever seen anyone who seemed so saddened."

Joan noticed that Miss Duncan was once more coming their way, the receipt for their hotel rooms in her hand. She picked up her purse. "I wonder if we'll ever see Yvette again?" she murmured.

CHAPTER 2

THE RIDE TO LAUPEN

Felica, Joan, and Miss Duncan left the hotel carrying their heavy bags and walked briskly down the steep Lausanne street to the railway station.

"We have eighteen minutes to walk three blocks, secure our tickets, and get to the proper track," Miss Duncan said. "If we move briskly, we should have ample time."

"If we had taken a cab," Joan panted, "we wouldn't have to move briskly."

"A Wellington girl never takes a cab for less than half a mile unless it is physically impossible for her to carry her luggage," the dean of women said. "A Wellington girl learns thrift."

As though to emphasize her point, she lengthened her stride a bit; Joan panted to keep up.

In the station, Miss Duncan deposited the girls and the luggage, then went to the ticket window.

Joan Bailey collapsed on the nearest bench. "If Yvette what-ever-her-name-is had been with us coming down from the hotel, I think I'd have asked to ride her dog," she said.

"You might get the chance at that," Felicia said. In spite of herself, excitement crept into her voice. "Just look over there!"

Joan almost cried aloud. "What a coincidence this is!" she said. "First we learn that she's going up to the same school we are. Now we see her in the station, so she must be taking the same train."

The tall, dark-haired young woman walked regally to the ticket window, the big dog just beyond her fingertips.

"That probably isn't as much of a coincidence as it appears to be," Felicia said. "She met her aunt in the lobby of the hotel near the railway station. The chances are she came in by train, met her Aunt Esther, and is going on by train."

Miss Duncan came bouncing back to them. "We must hurry, girls. Swiss trains are punctual. No time for dallying."

She snatched up her bag and started for the sub-way that led to the proper track. She moved briskly and with only enough reserve to keep her dignity.

The girl Yvette came up from the subway as the train pulled in.

"Let's get in the same compartment with her if we can," Felicia whispered.

Joan Bailey nodded agreement. She moved unobtrusively in front of Miss Duncan as they boarded the second-class coach and made her way to the compartment where the dark-haired girl was sitting.

"*Bonjour,*" the Bailey girl said, smiling warmly.

Yvette looked up and put on a smile but with some deliberation, it seemed to Felicia. "Good morning."

"Oh, you speak English," the Cartright girl exclaimed. "How nice."

Miss Duncan sent a quick, disapproving look in the girls' direction.

"Is the rest of this compartment taken?" Felicia asked.

"Not at all. I'd be happy to have you."

The strange, haunting sadness came back to her eyes. "I–I don't like to travel alone, especially today."

Both Felicia and Joan noted the reference but gave no hint of it.

They stowed their luggage in the racks overhead and sat down. Felicia was nearest the window, directly across from Yvette.

"This is Miss Duncan," she said after a moment or two, "this is Joan Bailey, and I'm Felicia Cartright."

"My name is Yvette de Benoit," the girl across from her said, smiling.

The train pulled out of the station and traveled along the shore of Lake Geneva, gathering speed as it went. The mountains rose across the lake in a majestic, breath-taking sweep that left Felicia wordless.

Clouds shrouded the upper reaches of the peaks, and huge white flakes drifted down to rest on the drifts of earlier snows.

"Beautiful, isn't it?" Felicia said to the girl across from her.

"I've been over this route a hundred times," Yvette said, "and the mountains seem more wonderful every time."

Neither spoke again until they were out of Lausanne.

"We saw you at the hotel a little while ago, Yvette," Joan Bailey said.

Yvette's cheeks tinged slightly with crimson. "I thought I saw you in the lobby," she acknowledged.

"That dog of yours is magnificent," Joan continued. "The St. Bernard is my favorite breed."

Yvette's smile came back again. "Blaze means a great deal to me," she said. "He belonged to my father."

"I see."

Silence came again and lingered.

"We're going up to Alpine Vista" Felicia said after a time, "to see Sarah Coulter, an old schoolmate of Miss Duncan's."

"How interesting," Yvette replied. "That's where I'm going."

Joan Bailey surveyed her quizzically. "You aren't going there as a student, are you?" she asked.

Miss Duncan's frown deepened. "Joan," she admonished.

"No," Yvette answered, smiling. "I'm not going

to Alpine Vista as a student. I've already spent some time there in the classroom."

"Surely not homecoming week," the Bailey girl continued.

"Joan," Miss Duncan whispered, "that is quite enough." She intended to speak so softly that only Joan heard, but Yvette de Benoit understood what she had said. The sparkle in her eyes revealed it.

"As a matter of fact," she said, "I'm being interviewed for a position on the staff."

Miss Duncan's interest was kindled now. "How fascinating," she said. "I teach at a girls' school too. What will your subject be? English? Math?"

Yvette's smile broadened. "There is a little academic work involved, but my principal responsibility would be to teach skiing and mountain climbing."

Felicia Cartright's eyes brightened. "Oh," she exclaimed, "how exciting!"

Miss de Benoit breathed deeply and toyed with the latch on her handbag. For a time, she said nothing. Yvette de Benoit was probably a few years older than Joan and Felicia, but she did not look it. Her face was small and pixie-like, and her short black hair framed her soft olive-hued face with delicate waves. Fire could kindle in her being and often did, but now her very manner suggested a bone-deep weariness that was somehow akin to dejection.

They changed trains in Montreux, and Yvette

slipped back to the baggage car to make sure that Blaze was transferred promptly.

"We were right, I think, Felicia," Joan whispered as soon as the other girl was gone. "There is something troubling her."

Miss Duncan fastened an icy stare on Joan.

"Miss Bailey," she said, "It is a sign of good breeding not to ask embarrassing questions and to be discreet in the way you channel conversation."

"I'm sorry, Miss Duncan," Joan answered. "But Felicia and I have been so curious that I just couldn't keep still."

"Restraint and self-discipline are the marks of a Wellington girl," Miss Duncan said severely. Then a strange light came into her eyes. "But the girl is sad – very sad. Something is troubling her deeply."

"If we could only find out what it is," Felicia said, "perhaps we could help her."

"Now, Felicia," the dean of women said primly, "a healthy curiosity is beneficial and desirable providing it is coupled with wisdom and good breeding. We must remember it is both rude and unladylike to pry."

The train whistled, and Miss de Benoit came aboard and made her way to the compartment where the girls were sitting. She took her place on the bench across from them and lapsed into silence. Her attention turned to the frost-etched window, but it seemed to Felicia that she was not really seeing the snow-shrouded chalets or the sharp, granite spines of the peaks beyond. There was a dull, preoccupied stare in her eyes.

As they drew closer to Laupen, the little Swiss village below Alpine Vista, Yvette's nervousness increased. She shifted positions uneasily from time to time, wiping the moisture from her hands.

Once or twice, Felicia started to speak, but Yvette's manner stayed her.

At last, the sturdy train groaned to a stop at the Laupen station, and Yvette got to her feet. "This is where we get off," she said. "Do you have someone coming to meet you?"

"I–I think so," Felicia replied.

"Yes," Miss Duncan said. "Sarah will be here. Even as a girl, she was very dependable."

Miss Coulter was waiting for them on the platform. She came to Miss Duncan, kissed her lightly on the cheek, and held out her hand to Felicia and Joan. Miss Duncan introduced them.

"And this," Miss Duncan said, turning to the tall, young woman who had ridden with them on the train, "is Miss Yvette de Benoit. She has come to be interviewed as a possible member of the Alpine Vista staff."

"Miss de Benoit," Sarah Coulter said, turning the name on her tongue as though there was some special significance to it. "Miss de Benoit. I'm so glad to meet you."

Felicia, who was watching both of them, thought she saw twin spots of color in Yvette's olive cheeks, but she could not be sure.

For an instant, there was silence between them.

Another girl about Miss de Benoit's age got off the train and approached them airily.

"Why Yvette!" she exclaimed. "I didn't know you were on the same train."

"Yes," Yvette said. "I am to meet with the superintendent and the board of directors too."

"I didn't think of that."

The newcomer turned to look at Felicia and Joan appraisingly. "I don't believe I've met your friends," she said. She was as short as Joan, very blond, and modestly dressed.

"I'm sorry," Yvette said. She introduced them one by one.

"My name is Winifred Sommers," the newcomer repeated. Her manner was cordial enough, but there was a studied air about it, as though it was a commodity to be used or not used as the occasion demanded. It went no deeper, perhaps, than the smile on her lips or the affected flutter of her hands.

"My name is Winifred," she repeated, "but my friends all call me Winnie." She turned once more to Yvette. "Can you imagine anything so unusual? Yvette and I both went to school here at Alpine Vista and were roommates at college. Now we're both being considered for the same position on the staff."

She laughed at the humor of the situation.

"At least we will keep it in the family."

The smile on Yvette's face was forced.

CHAPTER 3

MYSTERY IN THE AIR

In a moment or two, the bus to Alpine Vista pulled up before the station, and the girls got in. Winifred Sommers crowded ahead of Yvette and pushed her way to a seat near the window.

"It's magnificent!" she exclaimed, surveying the snow and the dark, forbidding crags that all but lose form and substance in the clouds. "It's absolutely magnificent!"

She turned to Miss Coulter.

"I don't know why I feel this way. I've been up here often enough when I was going to school. This place always brings a lump to my throat."

"It affected me the same way the first time I saw it," Sarah Coulter replied.

Yvette de Benoit scarcely heard what was being said. Her gaze fastened on each chalet in turn, each bend in the narrow mountain road, each graceful pair of trails that marked some skier's breath-taking descent. Her lips parted slightly, and a half smile lingered there. Talk, she could not. The trip from the railway station at Laupen to Alpine Vista had always seemed endless to her as a child; now it ended too soon. The bus stopped. She drew her coat around her and got to her feet.

"Is this the school?" Joan Bailey asked, looking out at the big, three-story chalet.

"This is the inn," Miss Coulter explained. "It's where the guests stay."

The slight, balding proprietor came to the door. Then, seeing that there were guests, he ducked inside for his heavy coat.

"Mr. Treveux!" Winnie squealed delightedly. "I haven't seen him in years!"

Before they could pick up their luggage, he came hurrying down the steps. "Good afternoon," he said in stilted English. "Welcome to our mountains!"

Winifred Sommers looked at him, a smile playing on the corners of her mouth. "Don't you remember me, Mr. Treveux?" she asked.

He gathered up as much luggage as he could, studying Winnie's face intently. "I should know you. Don't tell me; let me guess."

They started to move toward the inn with its exquisitely executed wood carvings.

The proprietor's high forehead wrinkled. "Of

course, you went to Alpine Vista to school. That much I know."

Winnie's smile broadened. "We used to come over and eat fondue whenever we could get the necessary francs together."

He returned her smile. "I am sorry, Mademoiselle, but all of the girls who go to school at Alpine Vista come over to eat fondue whenever they can get enough money together." He shook his head. "It is no use. There have been too many girls here at Alpine Vista in the past fifteen years."

She held out her hand. "I'm Winifred Sommers."

Monsieur Treveux frowned and then smiled his recognition. "Of course–of course!" he said. "How could I ever forget you? You were the little girl who always beat the men on the ski jump and climbed higher than anyone else." He set down the suitcases and pumped her hand once more, vigorously. "It is always good when our girls come back."

She flashed him a quick smile. "And this is Yvette de Benoit," she said. "You remember her, don't you?"

A strange light came in Antoine Treveux's eyes, and his mouth narrowed. "De Benoit," he said, his body tensing. "André de Benoit's daughter?"

Yvette's head came up, and her eyes met his. Pride stood full in them and courage. "I am," she said clearly.

It was Monsieur Treveux who was flustered. He fumbled with the bags, almost dropping one. "How interesting," he murmured. "How very interesting."

He started up the steps. "If you will follow me, I will show you to your rooms."

At the door to the room Joan and Felicia were sharing, Yvette turned to them. "It's almost time for tea," she said. "Would you care to go down with me?"

"Sounds great," Joan said. "We'll be ready as soon as we leave our bags."

A few minutes later, the three of them went down to the lobby together.

"This is a beautiful inn," Felicia said, taking a chair before the huge, open fireplace.

"My father used to bring me here often when I was a little girl," volunteered Yvette.

Monsieur Treveux brought them their tea. When he was gone, Joan Bailey spoke. "It seems strange to me that you and Winnie Sommers would both apply for the same school," she said. "Especially since you were roommates and everything."

"I suppose it isn't, really," Yvette said, a trace of concern in her voice. "Winnie always loved it here, and I–I–" There followed a strained silence.

Felicia and Joan felt the tension.

Yvette de Benoit studied her new friends carefully. Then with the deliberation of one doing what had to be done, she forced a smile to her wan face.

It was no coincidence that both had come to Alpine Vista to see about the opening. The notice had been in the school paper they both received. Yvette had decided almost immediately and sat down to write her application.

If the situation had been reversed, she knew only too well that she wouldn't be here now. But with Winifred it was different. She wasn't accustomed to being denied anything.

Something within Yvette died when Winnie decided that she, too, was going after the position. The papers all had written of Yvette's friend's prowess on skis and the peaks above Aletsch glacier in French-speaking Switzerland.

It was Winnie who had climbed to the crest of the Wetterhorn and the Fiescherhoerner. It was she who had won the skiing championship for Alpine Vista, practically single-handed, and whose gold medals were still accorded a place of honor in the trophy case. Yvette de Benoit took a deep breath. She could teach skiing and mountain climbing as well as anyone. She had learned the fundamentals and had learned them well. But how could she compete against Winnie?

In a moment or two, Winifred Sommers came down the stairs and over to the place where they were sitting. "So you've already had your tea," she said. "You're learning our ways fast." She pulled up a chair and sat down. "Not that I'm English. I'm as American as Yankee Doodle. But Dad's business has kept him over here for years." She paused and changed the subject abruptly.

"I suppose Yvette has already filled you in on Alpine Vista," she said, her voice cheery. "And that it's the best English-speaking girls' school in all of Switzerland."

"'Or the continent, for that matter,'" Yvette added impishly. "Remember how Dr. Dwyer used to say that?"

Winnie laughed. "I can still hear him. His voice used to boom like a Swiss yodeler."

"It is a good school," Yvette countered. "An excellent school."

Winnie nodded. "And the longer I'm away from it, the more I've come to appreciate it and the things they tried to do with me and for me." She looked at her watch. "Oh, I'm late now. I'll see you all at dinner."

Like a sudden spring storm, she had swirled in, rested briefly, and now was gone.

"Now you've seen Winnie," Yvette said.

"You know," Joan Bailey answered a moment later, "you can't help liking her in spite of–" She bit her tongue.

"Yes?" Yvette's eyes met hers.

The ornate clock on the wall behind them began to chime musically. Joan Bailey waited until the last tone had died away before she looked at Miss de Benoit again. The question still stood in her eyes.

"I didn't intend to say that," Joan went on. "Miss Duncan is always accusing me of opening my big mouth and saying things I shouldn't. I know it's none of my business." She paused and looked helplessly at Felicia. "All right," she blurted. "I will tell you I think it's horrid for anyone to do a sneaky thing like applying for the same position her best friend has applied for."

Joan stopped, and a crooked smile softened the sudden outburst. "But in spite of that, you can't help liking Winnie."

"She's really a very lovely person," Yvette said loyally. "I would have to say she's my closest friend and has been ever since we met here at Alpine Vista. She's very talented. Honestly, she has much more ability than I do."

"Just the same," Felicia told her, "we're both pulling for you."

Yvette smiled gratefully. "Thank you," she said. "Thank you very much."

They finished their tea and went back to their rooms.

Joan closed the door behind her and stood with her back to it. "Well," she began, "what do you think?"

"About what?"

Joan shrugged her shoulders. "About everything."

Felicia Cartright crossed to the desk and sat down, folding her hands before her. "I wish I knew," she said. "There's something mysterious, something in the past, and it seems to have to do with Yvette's father. Did you see the look on Monsieur Treveux's face when Winnie introduced her as Yvette de Benoit?

I'm sure the teaching position here means more than just a job to Yvette."

"So am I," Joan said. "But what?"

Felicia straightened decisively as she spoke. "That," she announced, "is something we have to find out."

They unpacked their bags, changed clothes, and wrote a few notes until it was time for dinner. They were locking their door when Miss Duncan came from her room down the hall and informed them that she was invited out for dinner.

"Sarah said you could come if you wished, but I told her I thought you would much prefer to stay here this evening."

"Thank you," Felicia said. "You and Miss Coulter have a good many things to talk over. We'd only be in the way."

Miss Duncan allowed herself one of her rare smiles. "I'm sure you have had quite enough of schoolteachers for one day."

"Oh, we like schoolteachers personally," Joan told her. "It's those assignments and classroom manners that throw us."

She and Felicia went on down the stairs to the dining room.

"The girls at home would consider this sacrilege if they could hear me say it," she confided in Felicia, "but Miss Duncan is really a good scout when you get to know her."

"I've always told you that," Felicia said. "She's strict, I

know, and a hard disciplinarian. But I don't think any of us have a better friend at Wellington than Miss Duncan."

Joan nodded. "I wonder if most Christian schools don't have at least one teacher like Miss Duncan."

Yvette and Winifred Sommers were already in the dining hall when the girls entered.

"Oh, there you are," Winnie said. "We were beginning to think that you weren't coming down for dinner."

"Miss Duncan met us in the hall," Joan explained.

In a moment or two, Monsieur Treveux brought them the first course. "I tell my waiters that such beautiful girls need my personal attention," he said.

Winnie laughed good naturedly. "You haven't changed a bit," she told him.

"One should never change," he replied, "when it comes to saying nice things to pretty young ladies." He then left as silently as he had come.

Yvette de Benoit touched the handle of her fork with the tip of a dainty finger. "I don't know what your custom is," she said, "but we always ask the blessing before we eat."

"So do we," Felicia answered.

They bowed their heads and prayed silently, each to herself.

"I was almost sure that you were Christians," Felicia Cartright said.

"And I just told Winnie the same thing about you and Joan," Yvette answered. "There was something about you that seemed to set you apart."

"This is nice," Joan said. "Somehow I didn't think we'd find many Christians here at the inn, even though Alpine Vista is a Christian school."

Winifred Sommers picked up a French roll and broke it in half. "That makes me think of my own experience," she began. "I went to school at Alpine Vista four years without taking a stand for Christ. The more they talked to me, the more determined I was that I wasn't going to yield. I didn't care what anyone else did. I wasn't buying any of that fanatical, religion business."

Moisture dotted her forehead, and she brushed her hand over it. Her throat tightened and her voice faltered, even yet.

"Then," she continued, "when I started rooming with Yvette at college, that was the end. She began to go to church with me."

"The Lord worked on you," Yvette corrected. "All I did was to talk with you a few times and invite you to go to church with me."

"That was all you did," Winnie said, "except to live a life that showed me every day how I ought to be living. A life that was so radiantly happy I envied you and longed to have the same joy and contentment you had."

Yvette's cheeks flushed. "You make me feel very humble and unworthy," she said. "I fall far short of what I ought to be."

For a minute, words seemed almost a sacrilege.

Felicia and Joan looked at one another and then at Yvette and Winnie.

The Sommers girl cleared her throat and forced herself to speak. "The thing that makes me feel so bad," she said, fumbling for words, "is that if it hadn't been for your talking to me, Yvette, and taking me to services and praying for me, I wouldn't be a Christian today. I didn't think I had time for the Lord until you came along. If it hadn't been for you, I wouldn't even be eligible to teach at Alpine Vista."

Her eyes grew misty, her voice faltered, and finally choked off.

"I'm certainly not sorry about that," Yvette answered crisply. "Even if it means that I don't get the position here. The day you became a Christian was one of the happiest days of my life."

Winnie Sommers breathed deeply. "I–I know I should go to Dr. Dwyer and tell him that I can't go through with it; that I wouldn't take the position even if it were offered to me," she said miserably. "But since I've gotten here this afternoon, I've suddenly come to realize that I want this position as badly as I've wanted anything in my life."

"You shouldn't feel that way, Winnie," Yvette said. "You have as much right as I do to be up here trying for the position." She smiled reassuringly. "Besides, if you weren't here, there would be someone else. So don't feel so bad."

CHAPTER 4

A VISIT TO THE AWARD ROOM

Winifred Sommers changed the subject suddenly. Concern melted from her voice, and she was bright and vivacious once more. "Maybe we could work in a little mountain climbing while you girls are here," she said. "I'll have to admit this is not quite the weather for it, but no one ought to visit the Alps without doing some climbing, regardless of the time of year."

"That sounds like fun," Joan Bailey said.

"If Miss Duncan will permit it," Felicia added. "You know how she is."

"You leave her to me," Winnie said, brown eyes sparkling. "I know about handling her."

Felicia glanced across the table. Yvette de Benoit was toying with her coffee cup in silence, a dark, pensive look clouding her face. She saw that Felicia was watching her and forced a smile.

Winnie was the first to leave the table. "I'm sorry I have to run," she said, smiling at each one in turn, "but I have a bushel of things to do."

"I suppose we should go upstairs, too," Felicia said when Winifred had left. "We've had a long day."

Yvette's gaze met hers briefly. "Don't leave yet," she said. "Please."

Felicia and Joan settled back in their chairs. Yvette de Benoit made no move to speak. Her shoulders tensed, and her arms, resting lightly on the table, grew rigid. The Cartright girl leaned forward, lowering her voice to a whisper. "Is there something wrong?"

Yvette rubbed her hand over her throat and once more brought her gaze to bear upon them. Her mouth twitched before she started to speak, and her breathing was rapid.

"I don't know exactly how to tell you this," she began, stumbling over the words, "but I–I cannot let you go on thinking that I'm something I'm not."

Joan and Felicia waited in silence.

Her eyes filled, and a scalding tear spilled down her cheek. She looked away and wiped them with her hands. Once more she raised her head and surveyed the tables around them, noting thankfully that no one else had seen her display of emotion. Slowly she continued.

"It's about Winnie applying for this job. You–you may think I'm gracious and–and understanding about it."

"We have remarked about that," Joan Bailey said to her. "I told Felicia I didn't know whether or not I could be so tolerant about it. I'm afraid my temper would get away from me."

The other girl tried to go on, but it was a moment or two before she could do so. "I don't want to be that way," she said. "I want to be truly Christian about it all. I don't want this to make any difference between Winnie and me, regardless of what happens."

"I'm sure you gave us the impression that you felt that way," Felicia said, "when you were talking to her about it a little while ago."

"That's just it," Yvette continued. "I actually felt that way while I was talking, and I was so thankful for it. But a little later, when she spoke so confidently of being able to handle Miss Duncan and get her way, my temper flared. I–I just couldn't help it."

She fingered her cup again without realizing it. "That's Winnie's attitude toward everything. She thinks she can handle people and get her way. And she usually does. I know that's the way she feels about this position here at Alpine Vista. I can almost see it in her eyes."

Yvette gestured helplessly. "I suppose that's why I sometimes feel the way I do."

"We can see how hard it would be for you," Joan told her.

"I don't want to be a hypocrite and pretend not to have resentment against Winnie when I do," she said. "What I really want is to be honest and completely fair. I want to be Christian about this matter. But this school means so much to me I–I'm afraid I can't be very objective."

Earnestly Felicia studied her face. "Is there anything we can do? Anything at all?"

Yvette struggled hard to hold her composure.

"Would you pray for me?" she asked. "Pray that I'll be able to conquer this thing?"

The girls both smiled their assurance. "Of course, we will."

"Thank you," she said without enthusiasm.

Felicia and Joan went upstairs together.

"Poor Yvette," Felicia murmured. "She's so disturbed."

"If they consider Christian character at all," Joan answered, "there's no doubt about who'll win."

Frowning, Felicia opened the door, and they went inside. "I can't help thinking that this other thing that her aunt was talking about is mixed into this school affair in some way."

"How? That's what I'd like to know."

"There are a lot of things I'd like to know," Felicia answered. "So much of it is a mystery."

"And one we're not going to solve tonight," Joan said. "Let's turn in. I'm bushed."

The next morning the girls expected to see Miss Duncan in the dining room when they went for breakfast, but she was not there.

A smile came to Joan's lips. "Don't tell me she overslept. That's one I never thought I'd live to see."

As if by prearranged signal, the door opened at that moment, and Miss Duncan and her friend entered. The dean of women swept the dining room with a glance, then approached the table, heels clacking on the hardwood floor. Miss Coulter was half a dozen steps behind Miss Duncan.

Her face was flushed and her eyes sparkling. "Oh, girls," she exclaimed, "you should have been with us. We walked out to the edge of the glacier to see the sunrise."

She paused dramatically. "It was magnificent! Absolutely magnificent!"

Horror clouded Joan's face. "At that hour?" she echoed. "Not for me!"

"You should try it. You have no idea how exhilarating it is."

The newcomers pulled up chairs and sat down.

"Sarah is going to show me part of the school as soon as we finish breakfast," Miss Duncan said, scanning the menu with a practiced eye. "Would you like to come?"

"It sounds interesting," Felicia answered.

Frowning, Miss Coulter consulted her watch. "There's not going to be much time before classes, but we ought to be able to see a building or two." She turned to the girls. "Which would you like to see first?"

"The trophy room," Joan said without hesitation. The teachers stared at her incredulously.

"The trophy room," Miss Duncan repeated. "That's a strange choice, Joan. A very strange choice."

"Maybe it is," she answered, "but ever since we've been here, we've been hearing about all the gold medals and cups that Winnie Sommers won while she was going to school here. I'd just like to see them."

A smile came to rest on Miss Coulter's lips. "I've shown dozens of people through the school since I've been here," she said, "and this is the first time I've ever started with the trophy room. But if that's what you want to see, it's certainly all right with me."

They finished breakfast and went over to the cluster of school buildings. Clouds had come up shortly after dawn to hide the sun, and there was a threat of snow in the wind. The air was crisp, cold, and invigorating.

Miss Coulter stopped at one of the smaller buildings and fumbled for the key. "The trophy room is here in the administration building," she said. "But I'm afraid you will be disappointed in it. It's not very large."

She opened the door, and they stepped inside. "You see, Alpine Vista has never gone in heavily for competitive sports." They walked the length of the building, and Miss Coulter ushered them into a small room that was lined with display cases.

"Your policy on sports is the same as ours at

Wellington," Miss Duncan said. "We are concerned in turning out the whole girl. A well-balanced, confident, gracious, well-educated, personable, Christian young lady."

"Even if it kills us," Joan murmured under her breath.

Miss Duncan pivoted. "Did you say something, Joan?" she asked.

Roses bloomed in Joan Bailey's cheeks. "I was just thinking aloud," she stammered.

They moved slowly around the trophy room, looking at the assortment of ribbons, medals, and cups that had been won by individuals and teams. Miss Coulter told them what each award was for and who had won it.

"Back about ten years ago something new was added," she said. "They started putting the picture of the student and the picture of her coach or instructor in the space on the wall above the trophies. And when there was a successful team effort, they had a picture of the team. "I think that's rather nice, don't you?"

"An excellent idea," Miss Duncan said. "It should help to form a bond between the alumni and the school, a bond that should be very helpful. And it gives the younger girls someone to look up to." She breathed deeply. "I think it is something we at Wellington ought to consider."

Joan and Felicia had moved a few steps away from the older women and were studying the awards.

"Look," Joan exclaimed, a moment or two later. "Here are some of the trophies Winifred Sommers won."

Miss Coulter came over to where the girls were standing.

"I knew I had heard her name before," she said, "but I couldn't remember where until I asked one of the teachers who has been here a long while. She was a very busy and very famous student according to what everybody says. I understand that she won all the skiing championships, and when it came to mountain climbing, she performed like one of the professionals."

"That figures," Joan said. "Yvette said she could do almost anything she set her mind to."

Felicia turned back to the trophies in the display case. "They have her picture on the wall," she said after a time, "but they don't have the picture of her instructor."

Joan's lips pursed. "That's strange," she mused.

"Perhaps they did not have a picture of her instructor," Miss Duncan rationalized. "Some people are shy, you know?"

"It is only for her grade nine awards that her instructor's picture is not on the wall," Miss Coulter informed them. "Here is the picture of her coach for the last three years, Mr. Gerald Fresno."

"Whoever her coach was, he must have been good," Joan went on. "Look at all the awards she won."

Felicia shook her head. "I can't understand it," she said. "I can't understand it at all."

They were still looking at the trophies when the door opened and Winifred Sommers popped in. "Hello, everybody," she said brightly, her best smile turned on for them. "I didn't expect to see you here."

"We'd heard so much about the awards you won as a student," Miss Duncan said, "that we decided to come and look them over."

Winnie was as happy as a child. "To tell you the truth, I usually manage to get over here for a few minutes whenever I'm here at Alpine Vista."

She went over to the case and looked down at her first medal. "I'll never forget the day I won that," she said. "I think it was the happiest day of my life."

She paused. "Excepting the day I trusted Christ as my Savior."

"They don't have the picture of your instructor on the wall," Felicia said.

The light in Winnie's eyes died away. Her voice, when she spoke, was thin and wavering. "I–I know."

"We were curious about it," Felicia said.

Winnie Sommers edged toward the door. Her entire manner changed. "I really must go," she said.

Joan's gaze caught hers and held it momentarily. "Is there some reason for the picture not being there?" the Bailey girl asked.

"I–I'd rather not discuss that." Composure gone, Winnie whirled and fled.

CHAPTER 5

THE PROMISE OF
MOUNTAIN CLIMBING

Miss Duncan went to class with her friend, so Felicia and Joan walked back to the inn through the snow.

"What did you make of that outburst?" Joan asked quizzically.

Felicia stopped and looked out over the mountain slope in the growing haze. The Wetterhorn was already hidden from view, and the clouds blotted out the peaks around them, causing the mountains to look dwarfed and insignificant.

"I've never seen anything so strange," she said at last. "What could there possibly be about the name of a ski instructor which would cause Winnie to act that way?"

Joan shrugged. "Search me."

They walked on in silence for the space of a minute or two.

"I was interested enough when we noticed they didn't have the teacher's picture on display," Felicia said, "but now I'm more curious."

Two or three hundred yards away they saw Yvette and her huge dog coming toward them, walking leisurely along the path from the inn.

Joan Bailey stopped suddenly. "Go ahead and meet Yvette," she said. "I'll see you after while."

"Where are you going?"

"I'll tell you later. I've got an idea I want to check out."

Before Felicia Cartright could protest, Joan had pivoted and had gone toward the administration building.

In a moment Yvette reached Felicia. "Hello, there," she said, smiling warmly.

"Evidently you're headed where we just came from," Felicia said. "We were going through the school with Miss Coulter, but she had a class and had to leave."

"I looked for you when I came down for breakfast," Yvette told her. "I was going to ask you and your friend to go with us. Blaze and I were going back to see how much the old school has changed. It's been such a long time since I've been here."

"We only saw the administration building," Felicia told her. "I think I could be induced to go back with you. That is, if you don't have other plans and would like to have me."

Yvette's smile broadened. "We would be delighted, wouldn't we, Blaze?"

The big dog looked up and waggled his tail slowly with the quiet dignity of his breed. His soft, brown eyes were almost as warm and friendly as Yvette's. And somehow they reflected the same hint of sadness. She reached down with a gloved hand and tangled her fingers lovingly in the huge St. Bernard's coarse hair. Blaze pressed close against his mistress and stood quietly, content just to be close. His mute devotion was unmistakable.

For a moment or two, it seemed to Felicia that her new friend had completely forgotten she was there. Yvette's lithe, supple body stood motionless, and she looked beyond her companion. Greedily, she drank in the mountain air, and the icy fire of it filled her lungs until they ached.

She was looking beyond her companion at the soft, white cloak of winter that crested the evergreens and masked the rocks and steep slopes in ever-deepening folds. She looked at the mountain peaks with their garlands of dark and ominous clouds.

"It is good to be back," she whispered softly. "It is so good to be back!"

Felicia Cartright watched her in silence, reluctant to break the beauty of the moment.

Down the trail a bell tinkled on the still mountain air; a cheery, silvery solo above the muffled whispering of the winter symphony.

Yvette turned toward the direction of the bell. Felicia did the same, and she saw a lone, well-fed sleigh horse plodding up the snow-packed trail. The tiny bell was on a leather thong around his neck.

A few huge flakes drifted down, standing in sharp relief against the dark stain of the chalet.

"It looks as though it could snow again," Felicia said, her voice hushed.

The smile came back to Yvette de Benoit's lips. "As far as I'm concerned, I think that would be welcome." Luxuriously, she drew her breath. "I used to love every minute up here. Even the blizzards."

"I can well understand it."

Her attention shifted once more to the school buildings scattered with apparent carelessness about the campus. Her gaze rested first on the old administration building. Then the library and the bright, new chapel standing out so boldly against the snow.

Yvette moved forward slowly, Blaze at her heels, and Felicia fell in beside her.

"I think I'd like to go over to the dorm first," the de Benoit girl said, her voice soft, as though still trapped by the hush of the morning. "I didn't get to live there very long. I stayed at home, of course, until Mom died. After that, Dad thought it best that I live in, even after Aunt Esther came to keep house for us."

Her words ceased momentarily, and when Yvette could speak again, all the joking and happiness had gone from her voice, leaving it dull, flat, and lifeless.

"It was only a year until he–until he was killed. After that I had to leave. There was no money for me to have stayed on – even if I could have brought myself to do it."

Felicia Cartright made no comment.

"When Aunt Esther and I left Alpine Vista," she went on reluctantly, as though some force was causing her to speak, "I thought I would never see the school again, and I didn't think I cared." She caught her breath. "Now I'm being considered as an instructor here. That certainly doesn't seem possible."

The dormitory door was unlocked, and the girls went in, Blaze close behind.

"Miss Frazer used to sit right here in the dean of women's office," Yvette remembered. "I was always deathly afraid of her, used to scoot by as quickly and as quietly as I could when her door was open."

"I know what you mean," Felicia laughed. "I used to be the same way about Miss Duncan when I first came to Wellington. I think it was two years before I got over being afraid of her."

They moved down the corridor that was very like the halls in the dormitory back in Wellington. Long, narrow, and dark and with doors opening off it at regular intervals.

"I'd like to show you one of the rooms," Yvette said, "although I suppose they're very similar to the rooms in your school."

Yvette de Benoit knocked speculatively on several

doors, but the students must have been in class or in the library. No one responded until at last they reached a room at the end of the corridor. The latch had not caught, and the door was slightly ajar.

"I think we've found what we're looking for," Felicia murmured quietly. "There must be somebody in this room, the door isn't locked."

"Either that," Yvette answered, "or there are some careless, young ladies who share this room. Miss Frazer used to take our privileges away for a week-end if she caught us failing to lock our rooms when we went out. I can still see her marching down the hall trying doors."

She rapped lightly on the door and waited. There was an instant's silence. Then footsteps sounded, and the door opened. A brief whisp of a girl thirteen or fourteen years old stood looking up at her, eyes wide with fear.

"Good morning," Yvette said.

"G-g-good morning."

"I'm Miss de Benoit," she introduced herself and Felicia. "May we come in?"

"I–I guess so." The girl stepped aside to allow them to enter.

There were two other girls about her age in the room. Books were propped open on their knees, and notebooks were scattered on the nearest bed.

"We–we were studying," one of the girls explained lamely.

They introduced themselves: Jane Wilton, Connie Harwig, and Ruth Mintzner.

"Our room isn't always in a mess like this," Ruth explained.

"You'd better not let Miss Frazer see it," Yvette warned in a soft voice, "or it's ten demerits just like that."

"Do you know Miss Frazer, too?" Connie wanted to know.

"Do I know her?" Yvette continued, keeping her voice down. "I'm going to let you in on a little secret. When I went to school here, she used to frighten me."

"Now I know why you're here," Jane Wilton announced. "You're going to be our new skiing and mountain climbing instructor."

"Let's say that I'm here to see about being your new instructor," Yvette said with a smile that won its way into their hearts. "I don't have the job yet."

Yvette and Felicia sat down in chairs the girls offered them. Blaze curled on the floor at his mistress's feet.

"Oh, I hope you do get it," Connie said.

"So do I," Yvette answered frankly. There was a kinship between her and the girls. Felicia could feel it instinctively.

"Are you going to be here long?" the one called Ruth asked after a time.

"I'm not sure just how long," Yvette answered, "but surely for a few days."

The young girl turned to her companions and whispered excitedly. "Well," she exclaimed at last turning back to Yvette. "It's all decided."

"What's decided?" Yvette questioned, her voice pleasant.

"We've decided to let you take us mountain climbing while you're here," Ruth went on.

"You've decided to let me take you mountain climbing?" Yvette repeated incredulously. "Now wait a minute."

"Up the Wetterhorn," Ruth Mintzner went on.

"Not this time of year," Yvette said firmly. "The Wetterhorn is much too dangerous with snow on it. A beginner just doesn't tackle a mountain like that."

"Who said we were beginners?" Jane Wilton asked indignantly. "We've been climbing all year. And we've made some real hard climbs. Mr. Bradford took us."

"But that was before he got sick and had to quit," Connie put in. "Since that happened, we haven't even had a chance to do much skiing, let alone do mountain climbing."

"Just the same," Yvette said, repeating her warning, "The Wetterhorn is one mountain you had better stay away from, either summer or winter, unless you have a good, experienced guide along."

The younger girls looked at one another petulantly.

Then Connie's face crinkled into a lopsided grin. "But we didn't figure on going alone, Miss de Benoit," she said. "We wouldn't be foolish enough to try that sort of thing. That's why we're asking you. We wanted you to take us."

Yvette's face relaxed slightly. "I won't make any promises about taking you up the Wetterhorn," she told them, "but a little climb does sound like fun, and I'd certainly enjoy taking you."

"Then it's all set!"

"Not so fast," the prospective teacher countered. "We'll have to see whether I can get away."

"You can get away," Jane Wilton announced confidently. "Anybody who wants to do it badly enough can get away to go mountain climbing."

They talked with the girls for several minutes before excusing themselves and starting for the door.

"I hope you get to come here and teach," Jane said, her freckle-sprinkled nose wrinkling.

Yvette put her arm around the girl's shoulder affectionately.

"I hope so, too," Ruth said, "and I hope you can take us climbing."

"We'll have to see about that." Yvette paused on the little porch just outside the dormitory door and looked up at the darkening sky. Felicia and Blaze stopped beside her, and the girls crowded close.

"I wouldn't want to promise about taking you climbing," she said once more. "Unless I'm badly mistaken, it looks as though we could get another blizzard. And if that happens, there won't be any climbing anywhere."

"There isn't going to be any blizzard," Connie informed her. "The sky has looked that way for a week. We'll be waiting for you."

Yvette and Felicia waved goodbye and left the dormitory. For a short time, they kicked through the snow in silence.

"You enjoy working with girls, don't you, Yvette?" Felicia asked after a time.

Yvette's young face beamed. "Oh, I do," she said. "They present a tremendous challenge." She stopped walking as she talked. "Just think, if I were on the staff here at Alpine Vista, I'd have a chance to work with girls like that every day. I could gain their confidence and talk with them about their personal relationship with Christ. I could help them to see how important it is to live for Christ."

She took a deep breath, and for the space of a minute or more, that distant, detached look came into her eyes. Felicia Cartright waited.

"I don't know of anything any more wonderful," Yvette continued, "than to have an opportunity to present Jesus Christ to those who don't know Him. Or to help young Christians with their problems and try to lead them into a closer walk with Him."

"When you talk that way," Felicia said, "you make me ashamed of some of my desires and ambitions."

A strange, hurt look flickered in Yvette's eyes. "Don't say that, Felicia!" she exclaimed almost fiercely. "Don't say that!"

CHAPTER 6

THE STORY IS TOLD AT LAST

Felicia Cartright and Yvette de Benoit went through the motions of visiting the rest of the school, but there was a strange barrier between them. When they parted in the lobby of the inn, neither said anything about meeting again.

Felicia loosened her coat and walked slowly up the stairs to her room. Joan Bailey was lying across the bed, her chin cupped in her hand. As the door opened, she turned her head impishly.

"Oh, it's you," she said.

"And who else did you expect?" Felicia asked her.

"To tell you the truth, I thought you had gotten homesick and had headed back to America." She rolled over and sat up. "Where have you been, Felicia? And what have you been doing?"

"Yvette and I looked over the school."

"You certainly don't act very happy about it."

The Cartright girl took off her coat and hung it in the closet. I'm concerned about Yvette, that's all." She sat down across from Joan. "What did you find out?"

"You'd never guess!" Her eyes were twinkling.

"Now you have got me wondering," Felicia told her. "Why did you leave me in such a hurry this morning?"

Joan Bailey's smile faded, and her face grew serious. "I went over to the library to check the old yearbooks," she said. "I had a hunch we'd be interested in learning the name of Winnie Sommer's skiing instructor."

"We are," Felicia said impatiently.

"Who do you think taught her how to ski and climb?" Joan leaned forward and lowered her voice to a taut whisper. "Yvette's father! André de Benoit!"

Felicia's eyes widened. "No!"

There was a moment's hesitation.

"But why don't they have his picture with hers in the trophy room?" she asked. "They have the pictures of all the rest of the winning coaches on display."

"That's what makes it mysterious," Joan said. "I asked the librarian, and she grew almost angry. She told me that they don't mention his name at Alpine Vista."

Felicia Cartright's forehead wrinkled, and the corners of her mouth came down to a straight, thin line. "That's strange," she mused. "That's very strange. It makes one wonder what he could possibly have done that would turn everyone against him so."

Joan got to her feet and crossed to the window where she looked out on the snow-covered slope. "Whatever it is," she said thoughtfully, "before he died, he convinced Yvette's Aunt Esther that he didn't do it."

Felicia came over and stood beside her. As so often was the case when they were alone together, neither spoke for a time. Felicia reached out with a slender finger and scratched some window frost lightly with her nail, leaving a fine line.

"It's no wonder Yvette feels badly," Joan continued. "I know how it would bother me if my dad was under a cloud."

The Cartright girl nodded. "She wants to clear his name," she said. "That must be one of the big reasons why getting this school means so very much to her."

The clock on the mantle began to chime.

"Time for lunch," Joan broke in. "Should we go down now?"

"In a minute." Felicia's voice was distant. "Do you suppose there's any way we can help her, Joan?"

Her companion smiled. "I knew that would be coming sooner or later." Then her smile vanished, and her manner changed. "To tell you the truth," she continued, "I've been thinking the same thing. But how are we going to be able to help her? We don't even know what happened or what to look for."

They went down into the dining room where they took a table not far from the window.

"Did you learn anything?" Joan asked in guarded tones. "Did Yvette give you any hint of what is troubling her?"

"Not at all," Felicia answered.

They leaned forward and spoke so softly no one, not even those at the next table, could have heard anything.

"I really didn't find out much about her," the Cartright girl went on, "except that she's a lovely, Christian person with a real concern for souls, and she has a love for kids."

"They like her, too," Joan broke in.

"You should have seen the way the girls in the dorm took to her. She had them so completely, she could probably have gotten them to do anything she asked them. And they had only known her a few minutes."

"I can understand that," Joan Bailey said. "I think she's one of the sweetest, most kind persons I've ever known."

Felicia would have replied, but Monsieur Treveux was standing at her elbow. He took their order, smiling graciously.

"Your friends, they are not here yet, no?" he said.

"We rather thought they would be down for lunch by this time," Felicia told him. "Probably they'll be along a bit later."

"I watch for Miss Sommers," he assured her, "and I bring her to your table so soon as she comes in."

"Thank you."

He checked the order again, expertly. "She is one splendeed girl," he added, "and on skis, she is as graceful as a swan."

He was back in the kitchen when the man sitting behind Joan facing the window, half stood and pointed. "Look!" he exclaimed loudly.

Everyone whirled to stare in the direction he was pointing.

"It has been years since anyone tried to climb that face of the Fiescherhoerner in winter!"

"Not since André de Benoit," someone else said quietly.

Jane and Felicia were startled at the name of Yvette's father and looked at one another incredulously.

"Not since André," another voice acknowledged. "But, of course, there has never been another climber like him. And I don't think there ever will be – in spite of what happened."

Joan and Felicia got to their feet and joined the crowd at the window. Two or three minutes passed while they stared in silence at the dark speck against the white of the snow.

"Treveux," an authoritative voice called, "would you please bring your binoculars?"

The girls glanced in the direction of the speaker. He was a slight, waspish individual with white hair and a scraggly moustache. Somehow, he was the type of person one would have expected to be heading a school like Alpine Vista.

In a moment, the innkeeper came with the powerful binoculars and handed them to Dr. Dwyer. The school superintendent focused them in silence and, for an interval, studied the figure on the cliff.

"It is a woman!" he exclaimed incredibly. "And with such skill! Such superb skill!" He shook his head. "A woman," he mumbled to himself.

The climber continued to move confidently up the snowy face of the Fiescherhoerner, a speck of black against the white of the mountain to those in the dining room of the inn.

"I can tell you who it is," Monsieur Treveux announced triumphantly. "Without even looking, I can tell you. There is only one young woman who can climb that cliff. And she is staying here at the inn!"

At that moment, Yvette de Benoit came up and stood quietly beside Felicia and Joan. Curiously she whispered, "What is it?"

"Someone is climbing the cliff."

"Do you know who is out there, Dr. Dwyer?" the innkeeper asked again.

The superintendent nodded. "Who else could it be except Winnie Sommers?" he retorted. She could climb like a cat when she was going to school here, and apparently, she's been practicing ever since."

Yvette grasped Felicia's arm involuntarily and

tightened her grip until the Cartright girl winced. She turned and looked at her companion.

Yvette's cheeks were pale and drawn. In that instant, she seemed to have aged a decade.

"There's nothing more to see," Felicia said. "Why don't we go back to our table?"

Yvette moved as though to leave them, but Joan Bailey grasped her hand.

"We'd like to have you stay," she said.

Yvette hesitated. "I–I'm afraid I won't be very good company."

"We'll risk it," Joan answered.

Once at the table, she removed her gloves deliberately and folded her hands before her. Felicia noticed that they were trembling slightly.

Monsieur Treveux took her order, and she once more lapsed into silence.

"I thought no one climbed much during the winter," the Bailey girl said at last.

"They don't, ordinarily." Yvette's hands clenched tightly, and her usually mild eyes blazed. "Who else but Winnie Sommers would have chosen today to climb the Fiescherhoerner?"

She spoke softly, but her voice was harsh, almost venomous. "When the people who are going to choose between us are here in the dining room where they can see every move she makes? What chance do I have against a climber like that?"

She clenched her hands so that the cords stood out on them. "And he taught her everything she knows!"

The suddenness of her outburst startled both Felicia and Joan. It was reflected in their eyes.

For the space of a minute, Yvette stared at the tablecloth miserably. When she raised her head, her face was slate grey and expressionless. The life seemed to have gone out of her.

"I–I shouldn't have said that," she began brokenly. "Will you please forgive me?"

Time seemed to stop.

"I keep fighting bitterness and resentment of Winnie," she went on, faltering, "and I pray for the grace to feel as I always have toward her, but it doesn't seem to do any good." The despondency within her tinged her voice.

"Yes, it does," Felicia told her.

"We're both praying for you," Joan added.

"Thank you," Yvette said, smiling gratefully. "Thank you very much. If it weren't for prayer, I–I don't know what I'd do."

Monsieur Treveux padded up to see what they wished for dessert. They ordered and again lapsed into a strained, unnatural silence but only for a moment.

"I know this is none of my business," Joan said brashly, "but you act as though there's something wrong. Something terribly wrong."

Yvette's shoulders straightened, and her eyes narrowed. "What do you mean?"

"We don't want to be prying, Yvette," Felicia said. "What Joan intended to say is that if there is something wrong and you'd like for us to try to help you, we'll be glad to do what we can."

"We noticed that your father's picture isn't hanging beside Winnie's in the trophy room," Joan continued. "He was her coach, wasn't he?"

Yvette de Benoit's lips began to tremble. "Yes," she replied. "He was her coach." She put her hands to the edge of the table and pushed herself back. "Thank you," she stammered. "I–I know you mean well and that you really want to help me."

Her words choked off, and for a brief span of time, she remained silent, her face muscles twitching with emotion. "There is nothing you can do. There's nothing anyone can do!"

Yvette got to her feet unsteadily, her cheeks showing with embarrassment. Felicia felt her own throat choke with sympathy, and Joan turned quickly away.

"Now if you–you'll please excuse me," the de Benoit girl managed, "I'm going to my–my room. I–I don't feel very well."

When she was gone and they were once more alone, Felicia turned to Joan Bailey. "You shouldn't have done that," she scolded mildly. "If Yvette had wanted to confide in us, I'm sure she would have done so. We shouldn't pry in her personal problems."

"I know that," Joan said, "and I didn't mean to pry. But she needs help. I know she does. And there's nothing we can do unless we find out just what is bothering her."

Felicia sipped her coffee. "I feel so sorry for her I can scarcely think of anything else," she said. "But apparently she doesn't want our help."

"Maybe she doesn't want our help," Joan Bailey countered, "or, maybe she doesn't quite know how to tell us or is afraid of what we'll think."

The Cartright girl returned her cup to the table and picked up her bag. "I could hardly stand to see her go up to her room alone, as disturbed as she was."

They were about to leave when Monsieur Treveux came over to their table. "I'm sorry," he said, "but was Mademoiselle de Benoit with you?"

"She had to leave early," Felicia explained.

He coughed and glanced at the slip of paper in his hand. "She neglected to sign for her luncheon bill," he said. "I suppose it is all right, but–"

"I'll sign for it," Joan told him, "Put it on our bill."

"That is not necessary, Mademoiselle," he said quickly. "I can send it up to her room."

"It's quite all right," Felicia put in. "We'll see her about it."

Joan took the pencil and signed the check thoughtfully. "You've been here a long while, haven't you, Monsieur Treveux?" she asked before handing the slip back.

He smiled proudly. "For fifteen years I have had

the inn next to Alpine Vista. And before that, my father."

"Then you knew André de Benoit, the ski instructor," she said.

Treveux's dark eyes flashed their scorn. *"Oui,"* he answered in hushed tones. "I knew him; everyone knew him."

"His picture isn't hanging in the trophy room," Joan continued, "even though he was Winnie's instructor. I've been wondering why."

Monsieur Treveux hesitated uncertainly. Felicia caught the strange glint that leaped briefly to his eyes. Was it fear? Anger? Or both? Color left his thin lips, leaving them blue and trembling.

"It—it is something we don't like to talk about," he said.

"Why?" Joan asked.

He moved half a step closer and lowered his voice so that even those at the nearest table would have difficulty in hearing. "It is a black mark on the glorious past of a wonderful school."

"It is strange," Joan Bailey persisted, "but Yvette is certain that her father isn't guilty of whatever *he* is supposed to have done."

That seemed to electrify the innkeeper. Crimson rushed to his cheeks, and his voice grew taut. "Not guilty?" he exclaimed indignantly. "Not guilty? He was seen on the cliff with the girls minutes before they fell. Everyone knows he was guilty!"

His face darkened. Felicia and Joan did not fail to note the change. "I did not want to bring any more shame to Mademoiselle Yvette de Benoit," Treveux continued in a hoarse whisper. "That is why I would not tell you at first. That is why the others would tell you nothing."

Felicia rubbed her fingers across her throat in a nervous gesture. She wanted to hear more, yet she dreaded every word. She had to hear more!

"Now I am going to tell you why his picture is not on display. He took those girls up on the north face of the Scheidegg Mountain in direct violation of Dr. Dwyer's orders. Then, when they got into trouble there, he panicked and started to leave them. Something happened, and all three of them fell and were killed!"

"Is that where he lost his life?" Joan asked.

"*Oui!*" Monsieur Treveux snapped. "But not in trying to save them. It was in trying to save his own precious neck." He glared. "That's why André de Benoit's picture is not in the trophy room."

For the space of a minute, Felicia and Joan were speechless. The innkeeper stared down at them.

"How awful!" Joan Bailey gasped.

"It is, indeed." Tight-lipped, he took the check from her limp fingers and bowed slightly from the waist. "Thank you, Mademoiselle," he said. "I trust that you will be descreet about what I have told you."

His gaze drifted to the doorway and froze there.

His fingers went limp, allowing a pencil and his check pad to fall to the floor.

The girls scarcely noticed. They were looking in the direction of the door at Yvette de Benoit, who at that moment loosened the top button on her coat and moved regally toward them. She looked at Treveux.

He laughed nervously. "Mademoiselle de Benoit," he exclaimed with forced friendliness. "You forgot to sign your check, and your friends here graciously took care of it for you."

"I was outside when I remembered," she said woodenly.

"If you will excuse me," Monsieur Treveux blurted, "I think I am needed in the kitchen." He fled before anyone had an opportunity to speak.

Yvette looked from Felicia to Joan and back again. "I remembered the ticket," she said, her lips scarcely moving. "But that is not the main reason I came back. I just had to see you!"

She swallowed with considerable difficulty. "I'm afraid I was short with you a few minutes ago. If I was, I'm sorry."

"You weren't at all short with us," Felicia assured her. "I shouldn't have blamed you if you had been. We were asking questions that weren't any of our business."

"We're the ones who should ask your forgiveness," Joan added.

It was almost as though Yvette did not hear her.

The de Benoit girl twisted the handle on her purse and bit her lower lip.

"Monsieur Treveux told you," she whispered coarsely, "didn't he?"

Miserably, Felicia nodded.

"But it isn't true! I know it isn't true!"

"Of course, it isn't," Joan replied loyally.

"That is one of the reasons I've wanted to come here and get the job of teaching at Alpine Vista," she went on. "I want to find out what actually happened on the Scheidegg that day. I want to get proof that will clear Dad's name!"

Joan's eyes brightened. "Can we help you?" she asked.

Yvette spoke slowly and with great emotion. "Thank you," she said once more. "But I've looked everywhere I can think of, and I haven't been able to find a thing." She spoke as though all strength – all hope was gone.

"Perhaps just talking it over with us would help," Felicia suggested.

Yvette was a long time in answering. "I don't want to burden you," she said finally, "but I feel as though I've got to have someone to talk to."

"You can depend on us," Joan said. "We won't tell anyone anything you choose to tell us."

Yvette de Benoit smiled broadly.

CHAPTER 7

TWO CLUES BUT NO HELP

Felicia, Joan, and Yvette sat at the table for a long while conversing in low tones. A busboy came and cleared the dishes. One by one, the other diners left until, at last, the girls were alone.

Finally, Yvette de Benoit glanced up at the big clock over the fireplace. "Oh my," she exclaimed. "It's already half past one and I have an appointment with Dr. Dwyer at two o'clock. I'll have to run."

Felicia Cartright laid a hand on her arm. "And don't worry, Yvette," she said tenderly. "Everything is going to work out all right. I know it is."

A sad smile slowly broke on Yvette's face for an instant or two. "I wish I shared your confidence," she said, "but I do feel better for having talked with you two about it."

"Is there anything we can do while you're gone?" Joan asked.

She frowned thoughtfully. "I wish I knew what to say," she said. "I haven't been able to find out anything so far that I haven't known. There has been so little written about it – a few newspaper accounts and that's about all."

She breathed deeply. "And no one will tell me anything if they do know." She gestured helplessly with her hands.

They left the dining room together; Yvette hurried up to her room. "I'll see you tonight at dinner," she called over her shoulder.

Felicia Cartright and Joan Bailey slipped into their coats and moved out into the chilly afternoon air. The wind had come up since they went in and was swirling tiny fingerlings of snow along the icy road.

Felicia glanced up at the Fiescherhoerner. "I wonder if Winnie got down all right," she mused.

"She's probably been off the cliff for an hour," Joan said cryptically. "She wouldn't have had to go very high to make the impression she wanted."

"We shouldn't say that," the Cartright girl protested. "We don't know that's the reason she climbed today. The thought may never have occurred to her."

"You heard her, Felicia," Joan said, "when she was talking about climbing and the school and everything. Doesn't this sound like the sort of thing she would do?"

"I hate to say that sort of thing about anybody,"

Felicia answered, "but I'll have to confess she does seem to be that sort of person."

They walked aimlessly up the trail toward the school. "Just where are we going now?" Joan asked.

Felicia laughed. "I was just going to ask you the same thing."

Joan kicked in the snow with her heavy ski boot. "Yvette says she's checked all the written accounts she has been able to find," she said, "so there's no use our doing the same thing."

"And it won't do any good for us to talk to the people at the school," Felicia added. "They wouldn't talk to us before. Now that Yvette has been asking questions, they're certain to be more close-mouthed than ever."

Joan grasped her by the arm. "Felicia!" she exclaimed, "I think I've got an idea! The people at school won't tell us anything because they want the matter to die and because they don't want to hurt Yvette more than she's been hurt already. But the people in Laupen will be different. And even if they do want to protect Yvette, they don't know we're friends of hers. They'll be more apt to talk to us."

Felicia's forehead wrinkled. "In Laupen?" she echoed.

"That little village where the train stopped," Joan went on, her excitement building. "It's only a few miles down there; everyone says the people are so friendly. We might even be able to find an eyewitness."

"Joan," Felicia cried, "you're a genius!"

Her friend smiled broadly. "That's what I've been trying to tell you and Miss Duncan all these years," she said.

They reversed directions and started walking down the mountain in the cold, crisp air. Its bite put color into their cheeks and frosted their noses. Felicia quickened her pace, and Joan reluctantly did the same.

Before they had walked half a kilometer, a bus came by; they waved it to a stop and got on.

"Now this is the kind of hike that I like," Joan said, sitting back in the soft cushion and closing her eyes.

At the first stop in the village of Laupen, the girls got off and looked around.

"Now where do we go?" Joan Bailey asked.

"One place is about as good as another until we learn something," Felicia said, turning slowly. Her gaze fell on a bright little chalet with an assortment of clocks and wood carvings in the window. "How about going over there? I've always felt that a person running that sort of a store would be friendly and agreeable."

"Suits me," Joan replied.

They made their way to the chalet and ascended the steps. A cluster of musical cowbells on the door tinkled cheerily as they opened it.

A thin-faced, balding individual stood behind the counter, smiling a greeting.

"*Bonjour.*"

"Good afternoon," Joan answered in English.

The man's eyes brightened. "Ah," he said with a heavy accent. "You are from the school?"

"Not exactly," Felicia said. "We just came up to visit friends."

"Too bad," he said, shaking his head. "Too bad. You would love it here in these beautiful mountains."

"We love it already," Joan told him.

They talked for a few minutes about the Alps, the exquisite, little Swiss valleys and storybook villages, and of course there were the inevitable questions about America. It was Felicia who first broached the purpose of their visit.

"Were you here seven or eight years ago?" she asked, "when the accident happened at school?"

The frown on his face deepened, "Accident?" he asked. "Was there an accident at Alpine Vista?"

"When three of the girls and an instructor from the school were killed mountain climbing," Joan explained.

"Oh, the accident!" he exclaimed, his eyes lighting. "*Oui,* I hear of it. But it was before we came."

He shook his head. "A terrible thing. A terrible, terrible thing." He eyed them curiously. "And why are two such pretty young ladies interested in something like that?" he asked. "Most people want to forget it."

"We would like to find out what happened," Felicia

explained. "Do you know of anyone who might know something more than was in the papers?"

"An eyewitness, perhaps?" the Bailey girl broke in.

He thought for a moment. "*Non,*" he said. "I hear some of the people talk of it when we first came. But none of them told us any more than you have said just now. And the past few years it has not been mentioned. I am sorry."

"I see," Felicia said, trying to mask her disappointment. "Thank you."

They left the little shop and made their way to the next.

"*Non,*" the storekeeper said in response to their questions. "I'm sorry, but we did not see it. In fact, we weren't here. It happened while we were on a holiday to Lausanne."

"Do you know of anyone who might be able to tell us something more about it?" Joan asked.

The storekeeper shook his head. "*Non,*" he said slowly. "I know of no one who saw it happen."

Then he stopped. "One moment!" he exclaimed. "Have you talked with Lucien Chalanda?"

"No. Who's he?"

"He has lived in these mountains since he was a boy," he said. "If anyone can tell you, he can."

"Where does he live?" Felicia asked excitedly.

"Down the path to the church," the storekeeper said. "Make a right at the corner of the church and go to the end of the lane. You can't miss it."

"Thank you," Joan Bailey said gratefully. "Thank you very much."

"It's only a chance that he does know something," the storekeeper called after them. "And if he does, he may not tell you. He's a strange one, that Lucien Chalanda."

The girls scarcely heard his warning.

"Do you suppose he really does know something?" Felicia asked her best friend when they were outside once more.

"He's the only real lead we've had."

The girls had been so excited, they noticed neither the clock nor the growing darkness until they were halfway to the church.

"I just thought of something," Felicia said. "When does the last bus go back to Alpine Vista?"

"I don't know," Joan said, "but we'd better be finding out. It's going to be dark in half an hour."

"And we didn't tell Miss Duncan where we were going. If we aren't back soon, she's apt to be terribly worried," Felicia said. "Maybe we'd better come back here tomorrow."

"I suppose so," Joan said reluctantly, "but I can scarcely wait to get to talk to this Monsieur Lucien Chalanda."

"If only it will help Yvette," Felicia murmured. "That's the thing that concerns me the most right now."

CHAPTER 8

FORGETTING ONE'S BURDEN TO HELP ANOTHER

I t was almost dark when Felicia Cartright and Joan Bailey got off the bus in front of the inn. Yvette de Benoit was standing alone in the snow, looking bleakly up at the Scheidegg where her father had lost his life. At the sight of the girls, she turned toward them and smiled.

'You've been down to Laupen," she said. "I wish I could have gone with you. As a girl, I used to love that little village. I thought it was the prettiest spot in all the world."

"I think it's the most beautiful town I've ever seen," Joan said.

The late afternoon wind had gone down early, and, though it was actually colder, it didn't seem to be. Felicia and Joan paused beside Yvette, looking out over the mountain slope as the lights in the scattered chalets began to wink on one by one.

"How did your interview go?" Felicia asked.

"All right, I guess." She shrugged her shoulders. "I really couldn't tell. Dr. Dwyer was cautious about giving me encouragement. But he was very kind, as you can imagine he would be."

From across the snow, a church bell rang out. Yvette stopped until the last melodious note had died away.

"He's not going to–to hold my father against me," she concluded. "He assured me of that. I'll get the job or lose it on my own."

Felicia and Joan were spared the necessity of speaking. Connie Harwig, one of the girls who stayed in the Alpine Vista dorm where Yvette used to room, had approached timidly a moment or two before and was standing alone, kicking in the snow. Yvette saw her.

"Hello, Connie," she said cheerfully.

"H-hello." She spoke uncertainly.

"Is there something you wanted to see me about?"

Connie's gaze lifted. Felicia and Joan both saw the disappointment reflected there.

"You're busy now. I–I can see you some other time," Connie stammered. Her gaze lowered once more.

Instantly Yvette de Benoit forgot her own problems. "We were just visiting," she said. "I'm sure the girls will excuse me."

"Of course," Felicia said. "We're going up to our room."

She and Joan went on into the chalet. When they were gone, Connie looked up timidly. From her own childhood at Alpine Vista, Yvette recognized that look, the pain in her eyes, her uncertain approach, and her obvious embarrassment. Something was bothering Connie Harwig. Something she felt she had to talk over with Yvette or someone. But she was not quite sure just how to begin or what to say.

Reassuringly, Yvette de Benoit smiled at her. Connie answered smile with smile briefly before concern drove it away. The older girl went over to her with slow, easy movements and put an arm around her shoulder.

"Now, Connie," she said understandingly, "It's not as bad as all that."

The youthful student pulled away and looked up at her, eyes blazing. "It's worse!"

"Why don't we walk over this way?" Yvette suggested, guiding the distraught girl around the corner of the inn and across the snow. "And you can tell me all about it if you'd like. When I was troubled during the time I was going to school at Alpine Vista, I used to go down to that big rock on the other side of the trees and sit behind it so I could be alone and think things out."

"You did?" In that instant, the bond between

them was forged stronger than before. "I go there lots of times."

Yvette's smile came back.

Connie's gaze sought hers. "Did you like to be alone?" she asked, almost incredulously.

"Of course. I think there are times when everyone wants to be alone."

The younger girl relaxed a little. "I thought I had discovered the big rock."

"And I thought I had found it," Yvette replied. "I suppose girls have been going down to that big rock ever since a school has been here at Alpine Vista."

As they walked, Connie seemed to relax a little, but she stopped with a suddenness that surprised her companion. She fixed her gaze firmly on Yvette's delicate, oval face.

"When you were going to school here at Alpine Vista," she began, "did you like it?" Anger deepened her voice.

"I didn't go to school here so very long," Yvette answered. "Only a couple of years. But there were times when I loved Alpine Vista and everyone associated with it. And there were other times when I'm afraid I thought I hated it."

Connie expelled her breath slowly. "That's just the way I feel right now," Connie retorted. She started speaking calmly enough, but as the words flowed, her temper took hold again. "It doesn't make any difference what happens here. I'm the one who's always to blame for it. I'm the one who is called in to the office by the dean of women. I'm the one who loses privileges and gets the extra work to do. I'm not going to stand for it anymore!" Her voice broke, and tears trembled on her eyelashes.

Yvette did not answer immediately, and when she spoke, she chose her words with great care. "You know, Connie," she said. "You bring back so many memories. You sound exactly as I used to when I was your age."

"T-t-then you know what it's like to get picked on all the time. That's what they do here at Alpine Vista. If something happens and they can't find out who did it, they blame it on me."

"I know I used to think I was being picked on," Yvette de Benoit continued. "Whenever anything happened and I was punished for it, I felt that it was unfair."

Her smile softened her words. "But as I got older and began to look back on the things that happened here, I began to see that I was really just feeling sorry for myself, and I deserved most of the discipline I received."

Connie Harwig shrank away. She was indignant and scrubbed at her eyes with a knotted fist. "I–I thought you would understand me," she snapped, "but you're like all the rest." Her voice broke, and she struggled to gain control of it. "And I–I thought you were my friend."

Yvette would have put her arm around Connie's shoulder again, but the younger girl drew away.

"I am your friend, Connie," she said. "Believe me, I am."

There was a moment's silence.

"Tell me this. If you were starting to climb a dangerous cliff that might give way with you, what would a true friend do? Would she sympathize with you and let you go on, or would she try to stop you?"

The tears were gone from the girl's eyes, but suspicion grew in them. "Anybody knows the answer to that."

"I've traveled the same route you're on, Connie," the older girl continued. "I've learned that all of our problems have a spiritual answer." She breathed deeply. "Tell me, have you faced up to your responsibility to God? Are you a Christian, Connie?"

Her young companion nodded. "They had a special speaker at the school last year," she said hesitantly. "I–I was converted then." She paused. "But I don't see what that's got to do with it."

"I'm sure you don't mean that," Yvette told her. "Surely you believe a Christian has an obligation to study as hard as she can and not to disobey regulations."

Connie shifted from one foot to the other and found something intently interesting in the snow at her feet. Two or three minutes passed before she lifted her head and spoke. "I–I suppose so."

"I'm sure you do," Yvette went on. "That is a hard lesson for us to learn, though. In fact, I'm still learning it."

"You–you are?"

"I've found that I can't hope to do it on my own," the older girl went on. "Paul in the Bible said that he always did the things he shouldn't do and didn't do the things he should."

"What chance do I have, then," she asked, "of living the way a Christian should live?" Despair was thick in her voice.

"The answer isn't in ourselves," Yvette said. "It's in Jesus. We should take our weaknesses and our stumbling to Him and leave them there. We should trust Him to keep us from falling."

Connie Harwig nodded. "I think I know what you mean."

Although neither said a word, they turned and started back toward the inn. Darkness was almost on them. And suddenly, Yvette realized that the cold had finally gotten through her heavy coat to chill her thoroughly. She quickened the pace.

They had almost reached the big chalet that housed the inn when there was a shout from somewhere behind them. "Miss Yvette!" youthful voices called excitedly. "Miss Yvette! Wait a moment!"

She and Connie stopped and turned to see Jane Wilton and Ruth Mintzner toiling up the trail toward them. "Hello," she sang out, waving to them.

In a moment, the girls had reached them. "Where have you been?" Jane asked. "We've been looking all over for you."

"Connie and I went for a little walk," Yvette said simply. "What is it that's so important it can't wait?"

"The mountains," Ruth said with a sweep of her hand.

"We wanted to find you and tell you that we're all set to make that climb tomorrow," Jane Wilton said.

Their voices were cheerful and lilting, but Yvette noted the serious undercurrent.

"I told you we'd think about going if we didn't have a blizzard," Yvette said, adopting their light, bantering tone.

"That's what you've been telling us ever since we met you," Jane countered, her disappointment evident, "and it hasn't even snowed."

"But have you looked at those clouds lately? A blizzard is due to move in any time. We certainly wouldn't want to be caught halfway up the face of one of these mountains by a bad storm."

The girls looked at one another in silence. "If you don't want to take us, Miss Yvette," Jane said seriously, "you'll tell us, won't you? You won't keep putting it off until you have to leave?"

"No," she promised, "I won't keep putting off the climb until I have to leave. I honestly want to take you. But we can't risk going if the weather is not right. It would be much too dangerous."

They had been talking so intently they had not heard Winnie Sommers approach until she spoke. "Now what is it that you're going to do if the weather is right?" she asked. "Who knows? Maybe I'd like to go along."

The girls turned and looked at her in silence.

"I'm Winnie Sommers," she announced, her voice rising slightly as she spoke. "Have you ever heard of me?"

Yvette de Benoit winced at the trace of pride in her former roommate's voice.

"Have we ever heard of you?" Ruth Mintzner echoed. "How could we help it? Your name's on half the medals in the trophy room."

Pleased, Winnie laughed depreciatingly. "I'm sure that's an exaggeration."

"Anyway, it certainly seems that half of them are yours," Jane put in.

The girls started moving toward the school dining room. Yvette and Winnie walked part way with them.

"Know something else?" Winnie Sommers asked. "I've got my name carved on the Wetterhorn. Right on the face of the highest cliff."

Disbelief showed in their eyes. "You–you aren't joking with us, are you?" Connie Harwig asked.

"I wouldn't joke about a thing like that," Winnie said carelessly. "I've done enough climbing on the mountains around here that I don't have to exaggerate. I just didn't dare tell anyone about it until after I'd graduated. We were forbidden to climb the Wetterhorn, and I'd have gotten sacked if Dr. Dwyer had found out." She paused momentarily. "That was before I was a Christian, of course, so breaking the rules didn't bother me any."

The girls studied her face intently. "Mr. Paxton, our other mountain climbing teacher, the one who quit last year, said that nobody from Alpine Vista had ever climbed that cliff. He told us it was too dangerous."

Winnie laughed pleasantly. "If you don't believe me, all you've got to do is go up and take a look. The initials are still there. I went up and saw them a couple of years ago."

Yvette glanced at her watch. "It's almost time for dinner," she said, "and I still have to dress. Goodbye, girls."

"Goodbye," they said, "and don't forget that climb."

She and Winnie walked briskly back to the inn.

"Did you have a good interview this afternoon, Yvette?" her roommate asked.

"I was satisfied."

Winnie bit her lower lip. "I can't understand myself at all," she said. "When I graduated from Alpine Vista, I was so sick of the place I thought I never wanted to see it again. Now I realize how very much I love it."

She paused uncertainly. Yvette glanced her way, a question in her face.

"I–I don't know how to say this, Yvette," Winnie

went on. "But I owe you an explanation. You're the very best friend I've got. You've done more for me than anyone else has ever done."

"Don't say that," Yvette protested, her voice thin and wavering.

"I mean it. And I don't want you to think that applying for the teaching position at Alpine Vista was my idea. If it had been, I'd have never come."

Yvette fought to keep her voice calm and free of emotion. "You have just as much right to apply for a teaching job here as I do," she reminded her.

"That's not it," Winnie insisted. "A person just doesn't do that sort of thing to her very best friend. I wasn't going to tell you this, but I've decided that I've got to."

Yvette waited, a new chill taking hold of her.

"One of the board members of Alpine Vista knows Dad well," she said, "and of course I've known him, too, for a very long time. He knew that I was graduating from the university and that the school was going to need a skiing instructor. So he wrote to Dr. Dwyer about me and asked that I be considered. Dr. Dwyer sent me an application."

She breathed heavily. "That's why I happen to be up here right now," she went on.

There was a long silence.

Yvette's head swam. So that was it. Winnie had been asked to place her application. She felt both relieved and crushed. Relieved to know that her friend had not voluntarily applied for the job. Crushed to consider the implication of Winnie's invitation.

"I–I would never have put in my application if it hadn't been for that," Winnie repeated. "But I wouldn't be honest with you or with myself if I didn't tell you that getting this position is meaning more to me all the time."

There was a long, unnatural silence.

"Thanks, Winnie," Yvette managed. "Thanks for telling me."

She stood alone in the snow until the door closed behind her friend. Then she half stumbled up the steps and into the lounge.

CHAPTER 9

PUZZLING INITIALS

The following morning, as soon as Felicia Cartright and Joan Bailey had breakfast, they went outside to wait for the bus that would take them down to Laupen and the old mountaineer's cabin. It had warmed, measurably, during the night, but the sky was still leaden, and the peaks around them wore clouds as a shoulder wrap. A few large flakes of snow sifted aimlessly downward, so slowly they caught in the air and were suspended there a moment before continuing to earth.

The bus drove into view momentarily and crunched to a stop before them.

"Now if Monsieur Chalanda is only home," Joan said, selecting a seat near a window.

"And if we can get him to talk," Felicia added.

The Bailey girl loosened her coat and scarf. "You

know, Felicia," she said, "the thought just occurred to me. We may be faced with a terrible problem."

"Like what?"

"What are we going to do if we dig into this affair and find that André de Benoit actually was the one who caused those girls to be killed? What will we do then? Tell Yvette and lose her as a friend as well as break her heart?"

Felicia pursed her lips. "I'd never thought of that," she murmured.

At the bus stop nearest Chalanda's little chalet, the girls got out and headed up the trail.

"Let's see," Joan muttered to herself after they had walked a few minutes. "We were told he lived in the last house. That must be it over there."

Felicia was looking at the little, square chalet that squatted so close to the ground the snow from the drifts and that on the roof all but met.

"There's somebody home," Joan Bailey said hopefully. "There's smoke coming out of the chimney."

They went to the door and knocked. No one answered.

"He's in there," Joan said doggedly. "I know he is."

Felicia knocked again. "What are we going to do?"

"You wait here," the Bailey girl told her. She plowed through the drifts to the back door where she knocked briskly.

After a minute or two, the door opened a crack,

and a thin, mustached face peeked out. "Go away," he said in French.

"But Monsieur," Joan protested, "we would like to talk with you a few minutes."

"I don't want to talk to you."

By this time, Felicia had heard them talking and came around to the back door.

"Go away," he growled. "Both of you."

"Did you know André de Benoit?" Felicia asked him.

The door opened a little wider. "Everybody knew André."

"Was he as good as they say he was at mountain climbing?" she continued.

He threw the door open and surveyed them critically. He was a wizened, weather-beaten little man, his hair and moustache as white as the snow on the ground.

"Better." He straightened a little. "There is no one who can climb as André could."

"Do you know anything about the accident that took his life?"

The light went out of his eyes. "I was the first to reach poor André."

Felicia's countenance lighted. "Then you are the one we have to talk with."

Reluctantly he invited them in and told them the story of what had happened that fateful day on the mountain.

"*Non*," he said hesitantly. "I didn't see what took place. I didn't even see them on the cliff, though there are those who did see them before the clouds blotted them from view. But it wasn't like André to take inexperienced climbers to such a place as the Scheidegg. It wasn't like him at all."

"What do you mean?" Joan put in.

"He was so careful," Lucien Chalanda repeated. "He was so very careful." For several minutes no one spoke.

"But you don't know for sure that he didn't take the girls up on the Scheidegg?" Joan persisted.

He shook his head. "*Non*. No one does." He got painfully to his feet and hobbled across the room. "But I have something here that makes me think he did not."

He took a yellowed newspaper clipping from the family Bible and brought it over to them.

"This was in a camera found near the body of one of the girls," he said. "It must have been taken a few minutes before the accident happened. It shows two girls and a man everyone said was André. They were on the cliff."

Felicia took the clipping with trembling fingers. "Why does that make you think it wasn't him?" she asked.

"According to the picture, André was climbing here," the aged mountaineer said. "See, at the far right of the picture."

"*Oui.*"

"But his body was found to the left some fifty or sixty feet away."

"Couldn't he have crossed?" Joan Bailey asked.

"There would have been no reason for a maneuver like that," Chalanda said. "No reason at all." He breathed slowly. "Besides," he concluded, "André would never have done such a thing as panic and leave inexperienced girls on a cliff, even if he had taken them up there. He was not that kind of a man."

Question as they would, the girls could not gain any more information from him. After an hour, they thanked him and made their way back to the bus stop.

"What do you think now, Felicia?" Joan asked.

"We really didn't learn much," she said, "except that Monsieur Chalanda doesn't think Yvette's father is guilty."

"But he said that he didn't have any proof," Joan added.

They walked out to the road and waited for the bus.

"The newspaper account mentioned that they were taking up a collection to put up a monument near the place where the girls and Yvette's dad were killed," Felicia said after a time. "Do you suppose it would do any good to go up there and look around?"

"It might, at that." Joan glanced up at the clouds that seemed to be thickening. "That is, if it doesn't storm."

"We can take the bus and get off at the foot of the Scheidegg," she continued. "We could be back at the inn before noon."

They did as Felicia suggested and made their way up the narrow, snow-packed trail to the cliff where André de Benoit and the three girls had lost their lives. The monument, a simple shaft of polished granite, had been placed on a small, level spot a short distance from the cliff.

Felicia and Joan approached it almost reverently.

For a moment or two, they stared at the memorial. Then they turned their attention to the sheer rock face of the Scheidegg that towered above it.

"Just look at that cliff," Joan said, almost in awe. "It's no wonder they got in trouble on that."

Felicia Cartright crouched in the snow and translated the inscription on the granite shaft aloud. "Dedicated to those who lost their lives on the Scheidegg the 3rd of November," she said slowly. "Amy Rollins, Marian Norris, and Della Sherman."

"And André de Benoit," Joan added. "They put his name at the very bottom, almost as though they didn't want it there at all."

Felicia nodded. "To the people who knew what happened, that extra space between the names will probably be very significant."

She stood erect, and Joan Bailey turned away, disappointment on her face. "There's nothing there that will help us," she said wearily.

"I suppose it was foolish even to think there would be. Felicia looked at her watch. "We'd just as well start back."

"We've got another hour until the next bus," Joan said. "Let's go over here and look around a little."

She led the way to the base of the cliff the girls had climbed.

"Now what do you expect to find here?" her companion asked.

"I'm not just sure," Joan said. "I've been thinking about Monsieur Chalanda and what he told us about the picture and where Yvette's father was found. If he is right, the man on the cliff in the picture wasn't André de Benoit at all."

"But it had to be," Felicia protested. "He fell here and died of the injuries he received."

"I know," Joan went on. "And this probably sounds wild. But suppose someone else took the girls up on the mountain, and Yvette's father saw that they were in trouble and went up to help them. The girls and Monsieur de Benoit fell, and the other man got off safely, but because of the uproar, he didn't tell anyone. That would account for it."

Felicia turned the matter over in her mind. "Monsieur Chalanda said there were a lot of clouds that day, so no one would actually have known whether there was someone else up here or not. You might have something at that, Joan." She expelled her breath in a sort of whistle. "But how are we going to find out?"

"It just occurred to me," Joan said, "that some people back home make a habit of carving or writing their names in out-of-the-way places where they've been."

They went forward and began to examine the rock cliff carefully.

"Here are some hand-holds," Joan said after a time. "They look as though they could have been cut several years ago."

Felicia went farther along the cliff. "Joan!" she cried. "Here are initials!"

"Really?" She went over beside Felicia.

"M. N.," the Cartright girl said, her voice quavering with excitement as she traced the shallow letters with a gloved finger. "See?"

"And here's another!" Joan exclaimed. "Here are others. A. R. and D. S." She stopped.

"What's the matter?" Felida asked.

For an instant Joan could not speak. She pointed to a faded A that had been carved to one side.

"What is it?" the Cartright girl repeated.

"An A," Joan said. "André de Benoit."

Felicia's face paled, and she felt weak and sick inside. "Then he was the one!" she said miserably.

Joan studied the space around the letter carefully. "The B. isn't here," she said. "It looks as though somebody took a chisel and cut it away." She turned to Felicia. "But it must have been Yvette's father! Who else?"

Felicia Cartright was looking down the slope at the dwarfed buildings of the school.

"What are we going to tell her?"

CHAPTER 10

THE SEARCH BEGINS

Felicia Cartright and Joan Bailey retraced their steps to the bus stop.

"I wish we'd never gone up," Joan blurted. "That's what I wish."

"We'd have never been satisfied until we did."

"I suppose you're right."

They waited in silence for the bus, and when it came, they found seats near the back.

"Been climbing?" a Swiss girl about their own age asked in French.

Joan shook her head. "We were up to look at the monument," she said.

"I see."

Once or twice more on the trip down to Alpine Vista, the girl tried to engage them in conversation, but they did not feel like talking. They were both glad when they reached the inn.

"What are we going to tell Yvette?" Joan asked on the steps of the big chalet.

"We can't lie to her," Felicia replied. "That's for sure. But I don't see how we can tell her what we found, either. I don't see how we can hurt her any more than she's hurt already."

They had hoped to go directly to their room, but Yvette de Benoit was sitting in the lounge. "Good morning," she said. "I've been looking for you." There was a smile on her lips, but her eyes were dull with sadness.

"My, it's nice out," Joan said quickly. "I just hope it doesn't snow."

"So do I," Yvette replied. "I finally gave in to the girls and promised I'd take them climbing this afternoon if the weather holds."

Felicia loosened her coat and sat down across from Yvette a bit nervously.

"I'm so glad you got back," the girl went on. "Winnie asked me to have lunch with her this noon, and I–I'd like to have you girls come."

"That sounds great," Joan Bailey said.

In a few minutes, Winnie Sommers came bouncing downstairs, her face a broad smile.

"Felicia and Joan!" she exclaimed. "How nice! Now we can all have lunch together!"

They went into the dining room and sat down. As usual, Monsieur Antoine Treveux came to wait on them.

"If I were you, Yvette," Winnie said, looking up from the menu, "I'd be careful about taking the girls up on the mountains. I was climbing yesterday, and with this loose snow, it's treacherous. No place for beginners."

Yvette nodded, and twin spots of color leaped to her cheeks. "I have no intention of taking them where they would get into trouble," she said. "If things do work out, I only plan to take them a little beyond the halfway house on the Wetterhorn. That's a simple climb."

"If the weather holds," the Sommers girl reminded her.

They finished eating and went outside.

Yvette's big St. Bernard got up from his place of vigil beside the door, shook the snow out of his shaggy coat, and came over to her. His huge brown eyes turned on her adoringly.

"If you take the girls climbing," Winnie warned again, glancing at the clouds, "You'd better not take them far. We're really going to be snow clobbered before dark."

Yvette de Benoit directed her attention toward the sky. The big flakes that had been falling intermittently all day had ceased. In their place, snow as fine as flour began to sift down. The clouds were huddling around the peaks, masking their upper regions in dark, filmy shrouds. The valley to the left was blotted from view with haze or snow. The warmth of early morning was beginning to give way, and the wind that was just gathering strength had an icy breath.

"It looks as though our climbing is already taken care of," Yvette said softly.

"I certainly wouldn't want to be up there in a blizzard," Joan Bailey said, shivering.

"Neither would I," Felicia added.

"You'd just as well go down to Laupen with me, then," Winnie said. "I borrowed one of the school cars to see if I have any mail."

"You didn't!" Yvette exclaimed.

"I have ways," Winnie said, laughing. "You should remember that from the days we were here in school together."

They were still standing there when Miss Frazer, the dean of women, came hurrying up to them. Her coat was only half buttoned, and Felicia saw that she was wearing no boots.

"Yvette," she said, panting heavily, "have you seen the girls?"

Yvette de Benoit stared at her. "You mean Connie, Jane, and Ruth?" she asked.

"Right. Have you seen them?"

"Not since last night."

The dean's face looked drawn, and perspiration rose on her forehead in spite of the cold. "They told me they had talked with you about climbing," she said. "I gave them permission, provided you went."

"They've been talking to me about it," Yvette

answered, "but I told them we would have to wait and see about the weather. Why?"

"They're gone!"

"Gone?"

"When they get back, I'm going to get to the bottom of this," the dean of women said firmly, "and find out why they have disobeyed."

Felicia and Joan looked at one another and then at the growing signs of the impending storm. Their arms and legs grew suddenly very weak.

Yvette's gaze sought Winnie's and held there. It was a strangely knowledgeable look; one that the other girls could not fathom. Winnie's gaze faltered and turned away.

The girls were gone! Suddenly, Yvette knew where, knew as surely as though she had been with them when they left and had heard their plans.

The night before, Winnie had boasted to them about how she had climbed the Wetterhorn and carved her initials there. They could easily have decided that if she could do it, they could do it too. Remembering the look of excitement in their eyes, Yvette de Benoit was more positive than ever of where they had gone. From the look on Winnie's face, she was aware that Winnie knew it too.

But there was no time to think of that now! Snow swirled along the path. In another hour, the mountains would be closed in tight!

"Is their climbing gear gone?" Winnie Sommers asked.

Miss Frazer nodded, imperceptibly perhaps. "That was the first thing I checked," she said. "It's gone."

She started away hurriedly. "We must get word down to the village and see that a search party is organized. There's no knowing where the girls went or how far they'll get before the storm breaks."

Yvette looked at Winnie and waited. The other girl let the dean of women start away without telling her.

"Miss Frazer," Yvette called out, finally. "Tell the search party that the girls have probably gone up to the halfway house on the Wetterhorn and turned left to the north face of the mountain."

Miss Frazer turned deliberately, her blue eyes cold and penetrating.

"Is that where you were going to take children to climb?" she asked. "You, who want to secure a position of responsibility on the staff? You are like your father."

Yvette de Benoit's throat tightened, and she pushed at her stocking cap uneasily. How could she answer? What could she say without getting Winnie in trouble?

"You can be sure that Dr. Dwyer will learn of this." With that, Miss Frazer was gone, running toward the headmaster's chalet in that strange, choppy little gait.

For a brief time, Winnie stared at Yvette. "I–I was going to tell her," she stammered. "I wasn't going to let it go."

"There's no time for talk now!" Yvette started for her room.

"Where are you going?" Joan asked.

"To get into my climbing clothes," Yvette answered quickly. "We've got to get to those girls as quickly as we can."

"Is there something we can do to help?" Felicia asked.

"We're going along," Joan announced decisively. "If the going isn't too hard, we should be able to manage."

"You can go as far as the halfway house, anyway."

They rushed to their rooms and changed clothes as quickly as possible and went down to the lounge.

"We must be a little ahead of Yvette and Winnie," Joan said.

Monsieur Antoine Treveux saw them and came over to the place where they were standing. "I would suggest you postpone your climbing this afternoon," he said. "We are in for a storm. A bad one, I'm afraid."

"Some girls from the school are missing," Felicia explained. "They apparently went climbing this morning. We're going up to help find them."

Monsieur Treveux's face went white, and his lips parted slightly. "No!" he exclaimed in something akin to horror. "No!"

At that moment, Winnie and Yvette came running down the stairs. "You three had better wait for the search party to form," Winnie Sommers ordered crisply. "I'll take the short cut and get to the girls as quickly as I can."

"The short cut?" Yvette de Benoit echoed. "That's only a saving of twenty or thirty minutes, even in good weather. With the loose snow there is on the slopes, it will be even less."

"But if they are in trouble, that can make the difference," Winnie said.

Monsieur Treveux stood there motionless. His face was pale, and his lips almost white.

"We can't wait here doing nothing, Winnie," Yvette said. "Not with that storm moving in. We'll start up the trail."

She turned to Felicia and Joan. "Is that all right with you, or do you want to stay here?"

"We'll go with you," they both replied without hesitation.

When they stepped outside, the wind was stronger than it had been minutes before. It swept across the steep slope, lifting new snow from old drifts and hurling it into the air.

"I'll wait for you at halfway house," Winnie said. "Or if I'm not there, look out along the cliff."

Yvette and Blaze took the lead, moving away from the inn and up the steep, dangerous trail toward the summit of the Wetterhorn. Felicia and Joan were a few paces behind.

"Did you notice how strange Monsieur Treveux

acted when he heard about the girls being on the mountain?" Felicia asked Joan.

"He was terribly concerned," the Bailey girl replied, "but I didn't think there was anything strange about it."

"Maybe not," Felicia said, but there was doubt in her voice.

Yvette quickened her pace, and they had to hurry to keep up. The trail was treacherous enough in the summertime, passing as it did along the lip of sheer rock cliffs and over the granite of at least one minor peak. A missed step at any of a hundred spots could send one tumbling a thousand feet.

Joan Bailey looked down gingerly.

"I don't know whether I'm as anxious to do mountain climbing as I thought I was," she said.

Yvette paused momentarily for breath, bracing herself against the wind.

"How much longer will it take?" Joan shouted above the shriek of the wind.

"Not long."

"Will we be there before Winnie?" Felicia asked.

"I don't think so," Yvette answered. "She'll probably beat us by a few minutes."

What was it her father used to tell her? She remembered it as though it were yesterday. "Never take more chances than necessary, even in an emergency."

"Are you ready to go on?" she asked.

"I think so," Felicia said.

Yvette made her way along the twisting,

snow-packed trail once more, her big St. Bernard with her and Joan and Felicia not far behind. She passed the first ledge slowly but with the firm, sure stride of one trained to walk the high places. Now and again, she glanced back to see that her companions were not in difficulty.

The ache in Yvette's heart continued to grow until it filled her being. The girls were somewhere up ahead. She had to get to them.

The ache in her heart was also in the hearts of Felicia and Joan. They moved forward cautiously, not daring to look down, driven by fear for the safety of Connie, Jane, and Ruth.

"We're going awfully slow, aren't we?" Joan shouted after they had been on the way almost an hour.

"That's the only way to keep out of trouble," Yvette answered. What she said was true, she knew. Trouble did come when a climber hurried faster than skill or conditions would permit, when he failed to check each step, each movement with painstaking care. But how could she keep from hurrying when time was running out? The storm could blot out everything around them in a moment.

For an instant, even the constant, wordless prayer within her ceased.

The blizzard that had given every indication of sweeping upon them seemed to have paused for breath. The wind seemed to have worn itself out, allowing the fallen snow to settle to the ground. It seemed to be growing warm once more, but Yvette knew that was an illusion.

"Maybe it's not going to storm after all," Joan Bailey gasped.

"Don't let this fool you," Yvette called over her shoulder. "The storm's holding off for a while but not for long. When it hits, it'll be for real."

"There's a chalet!" Felicia exclaimed suddenly. "Way up here!"

"That's halfway house," Yvette called.

The sturdy little rest house loomed ahead. Halfway house! And the girls were somewhere beyond!

The wind was beginning to pick up, blotting out the wooden structure with blowing snow.

Blaze whined and pricked up his ears.

"What is it, Blaze?" Yvette cried.

The big dog went forward, his nose testing the wind.

"There's smoke in the air!" Joan Bailey cried. "Somebody's in the chalet!"

They moved forward, and Yvette flung open the door.

"Miss Yvette!" a thin young voice exclaimed, "what are you doing here?"

She and Blaze stepped into the building, and Felicia and Joan pushed in behind her.

"What are you girls doing here?" Yvette demanded sternly.

They grinned up at them. "We got tired waiting

for you to bring us up here," Connie Harwig said, "so we decided to come on our own."

Felicia and Joan stomped the snow from their boots and pulled off their heavy woolen stocking caps. "Thank God they're here," Felicia murmured under her breath.

"It's a good thing you girls didn't go any farther," Yvette said. "The storm is about ready to cut loose."

"We know," Jane answered. "We were going over and see if we could climb high enough to see if Winnie Sommers actually did carve her name on that cliff. The clouds looked so bad we decided to wait."

"Winnie!" Yvette exclaimed, remembering suddenly. "Has she been here?"

The younger girls stared blankly at her. "Was she supposed to be?" Ruth asked.

"She took the shortcut, didn't she?" Joan Bailey asked. "Didn't she say she'd be here before we got here?"

"She should have been." Yvette spoke numbly.

"What's wrong?" Connie asked, getting to her feet.

The corners of Yvette de Benoit's mouth began to twitch. "That's what we've got to find out." She put on her stocking cap once more and fished her heavy mittens from her pocket.

"We'll go with you," Felicia said.

Yvette hesitated. "You had better stay here with the girls."

But Felicia and Joan both refused. "If you're going, we're going."

Yvette smiled gratefully and turned to the Alpine Vista students. "We'll be back as soon as we can." She started for the door. "Keep the fire going but be careful about burning more wood than you have to. We may need a lot of it before we get back to Alpine Vista."

She paused.

"Whatever you do, stay here. Don't try to come out looking for us. We'll be back as soon as we can." She glanced Joan's way. "Are you ready?"

"As ready as we'll ever be."

Yvette and her companions steeled themselves against the wind and choking snow and stepped out of the halfway house, Blaze at their side. For a moment, they stood at the door, breathing heavily and staring into the night. At times they could see thirty yards ahead. Again, not twelve feet.

"It's only a few hundred yards to the place where Winnie would have come up the cliff," Yvette explained. "But she won't be there. If she's in trouble, she'll be down on the cliff! Or–"

The words were lost in the wind. Neither Felicia nor Joan needed to hear the rest of the sentence. They knew, all too well, what Yvette was thinking. The same agonizing realization was pressing in on them until they were almost crying.

Yvette spoke to Blaze and slogged forward, the big dog alongside. She made her way along the steep slope to a narrow ledge with Felicia and Joan in single file behind her and the dog. Across the ledge, the trail widened but only a little. It would keep getting narrower and narrower until there was no longer space for a man's feet.

Yvette reached for the ice axe and *pitons* in sheaths on her belt. It might be that she would have to use them. And in this storm! A shudder ran over her! If that happened, Felicia and Joan would not be any help.

She moved forward with great caution. The trail had narrowed until Blaze could no longer walk at her side. Another fifty or one hundred yards and the snow had ridged over the ledge until it seemed to have disappeared.

Winnie wouldn't have been any farther away than this. She–

Yvette de Benoit's breath caught in her throat.

"What is it?" Felicia asked.

For answer, she pointed to the bare rock on the slope below them. "A snowslide!"

"What does that mean?" Joan asked.

"See that!" Yvette indicated a small ice axe to one side, half covered with snow. "That's Winnie's!"

"How did it get there?"

Yvette had to force out the words. "The snowslide caught her," she called. "It swept her off the cliff!"

CHAPTER 11

A NEAR TRAGEDY – A
TEACHING APPOINTMENT

A full minute passed.

A shudder not from the cold took hold of both Felicia Cartright and Joan Bailey and shook them.

Yvette de Benoit was motionless, frozen by the realization of what had happened. A sudden gust of wind struck the treacherous Wetterhorn slope, blotting out the dark gray of the rock below.

But Yvette knew what was there, as plainly as though she could see Winnie lying trapped in the snow.

"What can we do?" Joan called at last.

"I don't know whether we can do anything or not. You stay here!" Yvette started forward, and Blaze followed. She made her way cautiously downward around the fifty feet or so of bare rock to the edge of the snow.

"It's not any worse than what we've just been over," Felicia said to Joan. "Come on."

Yvette scarcely glanced up as they joined her.

"The slide wasn't very long," she said, as much to herself as to her companions. "We might not even have noticed it if we hadn't been searching for Winnie." She surveyed the area. Winnie could have gone the way she, Blaze, and her companions had come down. But she would not have taken the extra time to do that. She'd have gone straight ahead until the obstacles were absolutely insurmountable.

Yvette reached out and took up the ice axe that was lying half buried in the snow. Felicia and Joan moved close.

"It's Winnie's, all right."

"What could have happened?" Felicia asked.

"Winnie would have had to cut hand holds to go up the way she must have gone," Yvette said slowly. "She probably struck the ice with her axe at the very lip of the ledge."

"Would that have been enough to trigger a slide?" Felicia asked.

"It doesn't take much. I suppose Winnie could have done the same thing a thousand times without trouble. And then have this happen, apparently for little reason, if any." She crouched in the snow, a prayer unvoiced in her heart. The others did the same.

Blaze, who had been moving slowly as they talked,

stopped and whined. "Blaze!" Yvette shouted into the teeth of the wind.

The St. Bernard continued to whine and began to dig in the hard snow with his paws.

"Come on!" Yvette shouted. "I think he's found something!" She began to hack away using hands and ice axe alternately.

Felicia took the axe that had belonged to Winnie and did the same. Joan worked furiously with her hands.

"Is—is there any chance?" Joan managed, putting into words the hope that each felt.

"She couldn't possibly have been down here more than an hour," Yvette answered. "Probably less. It's—it's just possible—"

This was the sort of thing that did happen occasionally in the high Alps. It was one type of rescue work dogs of Blaze's breed were famous for.

The girls continued to dig frantically. The snow-ladened wind shrieked at them from across the barren reaches of the Wetterhorn. Their hands were numb, and their feet throbbed. They did not pause to rest. There was no time.

It was Joan who caught a glimpse of Winnie's bright yellow blazer in the snow. "Winnie!" she cried.

The figure below did not stir.

The girls dug with wild haste, then half-turned Winnie on her side.

"Winnie!" Yvette shouted above the howl of the wind. "Are you all right?"

Winnie Sommers's eyes opened and closed again. "Yvette!" she finally murmured softly, "thank God you came!"

"Are you hurt?"

Winnie moved her head in denial.

"At least I–I don't hurt anywhere."

"We'll have you out in a jiffy."

"Thank God," Felicia breathed. "Thank God!"

Joan and Yvette were both uttering a prayer of thanksgiving as they put their arms around Winnie's shoulders and helped her to her feet.

Winnie leaned heavily. "I don't know whether I can walk," she said. "No strength."

"We'll help you."

The girls took turns, one on either side of Winnie, and helped her across the slope toward a trail that was a longer way around but wide enough for them to negotiate without trouble.

The storm was building up. It choked their breathing and drove the snow into the folds of their clothes where it caked and froze.

They dare not stop! They were a hundred yards or more from the halfway house when the rescue party met them. Dr. Dwyer and a man they had never seen before came forward.

"Yvette!" the headmaster exclaimed, "what happened?"

She stopped and sagged wearily. She could not answer.

"Here," Dr. Dwyer said. "We'll take charge of Winnie."

They helped her into the chalet. Yvette, Felicia, and Joan followed, half staggering along behind.

Miss Duncan and her friend, Sarah Coulter, were there, together with Miss Frazer. Miss Duncan came to Felicia and Joan, deep concern in her voice. "Are you all right?" she asked solicitously.

"Just cold," Joan answered. "I wonder if I'll ever get warm again."

The medical doctor from the village, who had come with the rescuers, examined the girls. "Nothing too wrong with any of you," he said at last. He glanced over at a bunk in the corner.

"If it hadn't been for Antoine getting sick on the way up here, we'd have gotten by without a casualty."

"Antoine?" Felicia repeated curiously. "Antoine. Antoine Treveux."

At the mention of his name, the innkeeper moaned a little and shifted position.

"What's wrong with him?"

The doctor's forehead wrinkled thoughtfully. "I'm not entirely sure," he said evasively. "The higher we got, the sicker he got. He was so sick to his stomach that we almost had to carry him the last kilometer. I think he'll be all right now."

"Antoine," Felicia said softly. "Antoine! Why that starts with an A, too!"

Suddenly it seemed to fit into place. She sought Yvette de Benoit's gaze and, motioning toward the sick man, got to her feet. Yvette did the same.

Everyone else was talking so much they did not notice what was happening.

"What do you want, Felicia?"

"Just stand here and listen. I think I've got some very interesting information."

"Monsieur Treveux, is this the first time you've done any mountain climbing?" she asked.

He groaned for answer.

"I didn't think so," she continued, keeping her voice down. "We saw your initials up on the Scheidegg."

He opened his eyes wide. "I–I don't know what you're talking about," he blurted out.

"You went back and cut the T out of the rock, but the A is just as plain as ever."

"If there's an A up on the Scheidegg, it was put there by André de Benoit. Not me."

"That's what you have wanted people to believe," Felicia went on. "The truth is that you were the one who took those girls up on the Scheidegg. You were the one shown in the picture. Then, when they got in trouble, you panicked and managed to get down safely. André de Benoit went up and lost his life try-ing to help them."

"It isn't true," he countered. "None of it is true."

"That's why you've been afraid to climb," the Cartright girl continued. "You haven't climbed since that happened, have you?"

He did not answer, but she expected no answer. Yvette de Benoit was trembling.

"When we told you a rescue party was being formed to go up after the girls today, you were terribly frightened. You knew that you'd be expected to go along! That it would look suspicious – even after all these years – if you didn't, when people like Dr. Dwyer knew that you used to climb so much."

"No! No!" He spoke so loudly now the others in the room heard, and conversation ceased. But they were all so tense, they did not realize what was going on.

"That's why you got sick coming up here to the halfway house, isn't it?" Felicia asked. "You got sick thinking about having to climb again."

He did not speak, but by the look in his eyes, he confirmed everything she had said.

"I knew Dad wasn't guilty of leaving the girls on the cliff," Yvette murmured thankfully. "*I knew!*"

"What are you going to do now?" Treveux asked miserably. "Tell everybody? Ruin my reputation?"

She did not answer immediately.

"I don't know yet," she said truthfully. "I don't want to hurt you any more than you've been hurt. The important thing is that *I* know he wasn't guilty."

There was brief hesitation. Dr. Dwyer moved silently to her.

"That is one decision you don't have to make, Yvette," he said quietly.

Both she and Monsieur Treveux were startled.

"You–you heard?" she whispered.

"We heard! Enough! Enough!"

The perspiration stood out on Monsieur Treveux's face.

"I'm sorry for you, Antoine," Dr. Dwyer said, his voice hushed but steady. "Truly I am. I can imagine how you've tormented yourself letting the memory of a brave man be clouded by cowardice. Yours."

He took Yvette by the arm and led her back to the stove.

For a long while, no one spoke. Felicia and Joan watched their friend, Yvette, happily.

"Dad's memory is cleared," Yvette said, "and that's the main thing. I feel so sorry for Monsieur Treveux. He's hurt so badly by all of this."

"It was his own doing," Felicia reminded her.

"But what made you suspect that it was him?" Yvette asked. "He's the last person I'd have thought of."

"We went down and talked with Lucien Chalanda," Felicia said. "He's the one who raised doubts, first, that it wasn't your dad in the picture – the one the girls took as they started to climb. If that was true, it meant that someone else had to have been with them."

"Then when we went up to see the monument," Joan Bailey put in, "we found those initials on the face of the Scheidegg. We thought for sure, then, that your dad was the guilty one."

"It didn't occur to us that he would not have carved his last initial and then cut it out," Felicia said.

"I guess the thing that really made everything fall into place," Joan went on, "was seeing Monsieur Treveux sick over there then hearing the doctor call him Antoine! That's when it clicked!"

Yvette smiled gratefully. "I'll never be able to repay you."

"You don't have to worry about that."

The storm raged all that night. It was almost noon the next day before the wind began to ease and the snow let up so they could think about getting back to the school.

"I'm afraid we have missed our appointments with you, Dr. Dwyer," Winnie said, smiling.

"While I cannot speak for the rest of the board," Dr. Dwyer said, "they usually follow my recommendations. And I don't think further interviews are necessary now. I believe we have learned enough."

Winnie and Yvette looked at one another quickly and then at the headmaster.

"Anyone can have an accident like I had yesterday," Winnie said.

Dr. Dwyer nodded. "To be sure," he replied evenly. "And I want you to know that has nothing to do with my decision. Neither does your bragging about your climbing exploits and giving the girls the idea of climbing the Wetterhorn as you did."

He paused and looked Yvette's way. "Neither does the fact that Yvette promised to bring the girls up here, a factor which undoubtedly contributed to their decision, have anything to do with the way I have made up my mind."

He paused deliberately, then went on.

"The girls knew their restrictions. They should not have permitted anything anyone said to them make them decide to break regulations."

Yvette de Benoit's lips trembled slightly as Dr. Dwyer looked at her and then at Winnie.

"I'm not even being influenced by the fact that your father's name is cleared, Yvette," he added, "though I must say the Christian way in which you talked with Monsieur Treveux has served to make me more sure of my decision."

She stared at him incredulously.

"Winnie," he continued in a moment, "you have tremendous climbing ability and courage to spare. You are as skilled as any young mountain climber I know."

Winnie Sommers managed a faint smile. "Thank you."

"But," Dr. Dwyer continued, "we are interested in staffing Alpine with teachers of good judgment who have the best interests of the girls at heart."

She straightened, the color leaving her cheeks.

"You had to take the shortcut up here, dangerous as it is in the winter, although you could only have hoped to save a few minutes at best. But it was spectacular, something that made a hero of you. When you talked with the girls, you boasted of the things you did here, all of the awards you won, the honors you got.

"When Yvette came up here, she took the trail. When she talked with the girls, she presented Christ to them."

He turned to Yvette de Benoit. "I am going to recommend you for the teaching position, Yvette," he said.

Her head spun.

Felicia and Joan could have shouted for joy.

* * *

Back at the inn the next day, Winnie had her bags packed and was down in the lounge.

"I'm sorry we couldn't both have won," Yvette said sadly.

Her roommate looked up. "Didn't I tell you? We did."

"What do you mean?"

"I did a lot of thinking last night, Yvette. You're the one who should have gotten the job here at Alpine. You'll do more for the girls than I ever could. I mean it. You've made me see I've been selfish and conceited, more interested in giving people a high opinion of Winnie Sommers than of serving Christ."

She took a deep breath. "With God's help, it's going to be different. I'll take one of the other schools I've been offered and will be doing all I can to serve Christ."

Yvette smiled then thrust out her hand. Winnie took it warmly.

Felicia Cartright, who was standing nearby, turned to her best friend. "I'm so happy I could cry," she whispered to Joan.

"Don't you dare!" Joan retorted. "If you start, I'll be doing it too!"

THE
FELICIA CARTRIGHT
SERIES

Felicia Cartright, a petite blonde who is one of the most popular students at Wellington School for Girls, has a surprising inclination toward mysteries. If a mysterious situation arises, it either makes its way to Felicia, or Felicia somehow finds it. Though this is a bit trying for her happy-go-lucky roommate, Joan Bailey, it does prevent life from becoming monotonous. It also enables Bernard Palmer, the popular author of the "Danny Orlis" books, to write an entertaining series of stories for girls aged twelve to eighteen.

The mysteries range from a valuable missing antique to an attempt by claim jumpers to steal a deposit of tungsten ore. There's excitement and action galore—but there's also spiritual guidance and blessing because Felicia and her partner-in-adventure love the Lord and take Him into account in all their experiences.

AVAILABLE FROM WWW.ANEKOPRESS.COM

www.ingramcontent.com/pod-product-compliance
Lightning Source LLC
Chambersburg PA
CBHW071522120626
46550CB00006B/2329